Aberdeen:

D1420274

HISTORY /
SCOTTISH INTEREST

£ 8

(34)

Contents

Published by the
City of Aberdeen
Department of Information
and Tourism
St. Nicholas House, Aberdeen

❊

Editorial Written by:
CUTHBERT GRAHAM

❊

Opposite:
ABERDEEN TOWN HOUSE AND
SHERIFF COURT BUILDING
ON RIGHT

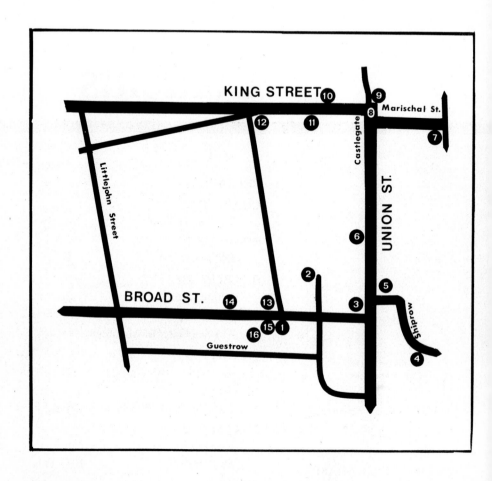

This Map covers Chapter I (pages 5-27)

THE ITEMS OF INTEREST DO NOT NECESSARILY FOLLOW THE EDITORIAL ORDER.

1 Information Bureau
2 Advocates Hall
3 Town House
4 Provost Ross's House
5 Mannie o' the Green & Planestanes
6 Tolbooth
7 Elim Gospel Church
8 Mercat Cross

9 Salvation Army Citadel
10 St. Andrew's Cathedral
11 Medico-Chirurgical Building
12 Arts Centre
13 Greyfriars Church
14 Marischal College
15 Provost Skene's House
16 St. Nicholas House

Preface . . .

THERE is always a difficulty in knowing where to begin. Did you enter the city by car from the south traversing the bare, almost treeless uplands of northern Kincardine and the nigh imperceptible ridge of the Grampians, better-known as the Mounth, and catch your first glimpse of the towers and steeples of the town spread out before you beyond the silver ribbon of the Dee? Did you come by train, hugging the rock-girt coves of the North Sea coast and spot the white pencil of Girdleness Lighthouse beyond the sandy sweep of the Bay of Nigg? Or did you drop from the clouds to the green, hill-guarded level of the Aberdeen Airport at Dyce?

Let us overcome these difficulties of alternative approach by assuming that you have reached the city centre at the eastern end of Union Street, the mile-long granite pivot of the modern city. If you have acquired this Visitor's Guide at the Information Bureau in St. Nicholas House it is only a step from the 15-storey municipal offices there to the ancient and historic heart of the royal burgh. Turn right when you emerge from the Bureau and walk southwards down Broad Street to its junction with Union Street and Castle Street. You will now be standing at the corner of the massive tower and steeple of Aberdeen Town House with its almost top-heavy Douai-style belfry. This building in a Flemish-Medieval style in granite ashlar, with arcaded ground floor, has been the headquarters of Aberdeen Corporation for over a century, having been built to designs by Peddie and Kinnear in the years 1868-74. But it fronts a very ancient "place" or open space, known for 600 years as—

CHAPTER I — THE CASTLEGATE

It has been the custom to say that the Castlegate of today is so utterly changed from its ancient forerunner that the only thing that remains is its actual dimensions — "a square about a hundred walking paces broad and twice as much in length" as Parson James Gordon of Rothiemay, author of the first "visitor's guide" to Aberdeen put it in the year 1661, adding with native pride "nor can Scotland show such another". But this is not quite true. The Castlegate is longer now than it was in 1661 and it still retains in stone and lime, buildings which carry its story back 350 years.

Documentary records take the tale much further back still. For the name Castlegate means the "gait" or way to the Castle, the royal citadel or stronghold which in the thirteenth century stood as the symbol of the king's authority over the royal burgh which he had established in Aberdeen at least as early as 1179. The Castle of Aberdeen was probably built in the first half of the thirteenth century. It stood on the Castle Hill, the site immediately to the east of the Castlegate now occupied by two soaring blocks of high-rise flats.

By 1264 the castle was in need of repair and the man to whom the job was entrusted was one Richard Cementarius — Richard the Mason, Alderman of Aberdeen, the city's first recorded Provost or Chief

On the 9th April, 1848 the barque "CARLETON" (Captain Hugh Alexander) set sail from Aberdeen bound for Quebec, the first of a fleet of sailing vessels and steamers owned by John Cook to do so during the next 80 years.

During these early years the firm carried on a tramp cargo business mainly to Scandinavia but also further afield in Australia and New Zealand. One of his earlier vessels the "FAMENOTH" carried many passengers, indeed emigrants to the Colony of New Zealand.

Exactly 100 years ago, there were 205 trading vessels registered in the Port of Aberdeen, and today we have nearer 20. Over the years the pattern of business changed and John Cook's grandson Mr. James Cook, was responsible for the sale of the shipping fleet to Christian Salvesen of Leith in 1928. Nevertheless they continued to be the main Shipping Agents in Aberdeen, especially associated with the Scandinavian trade. They also developed a business as Shipbrokers and general Shipping Agents, Stevedores and Marine Insurance Brokers.

With the decasualisation of dock labour in 1966 they ceased being stevedores but took over the managing of the newly formed Aberdeen Stevedoring Company, a service which they still fulfil. At this time Cook amalgamated with two other shipbroking firms, Richard Connon Reid and W. R. Aiken Ltd.

Until 1970 the firm was controlled and managed by the Cook family. At that date the controlling interest was sold to Christian Salvesen with whom a very close business connection had been maintained since the sale of the fleet.

The firm has seen many changes in the port of Aberdeen from the time of the sailing clippers to the advent of the new oil rig service vessels now plying between the port and various rigs in the North Sea.

Cooks have kept abreast of the times in supplying modern stevedoring equipment and are now involved in the offshore oil industry especially as owners and/or charterers' agents for the supply vessels. They have opened a Travel Agency Office at 55/57 Marischal Street.

As members of the Salvesen Group they can offer a wide variety of services in connection with shipping and associated with cold storage facilities, housing contractors and transport companies. Christian Salvesen now have an oil services division in Aberdeen offering sophisticated multi-purpose stand-by vessels, casing crews and industrial cleaning services.

The Property Division have recently built Salvesen Tower, an 11-storey office block on the quayside. This has proved to be a handsome contribution to the Port's facilities. As can be seen, therefore, even after 130 years the Company is still moving with the times and, if these have changed, enterprise has in no way abated.

Magistrate. Another thirteenth century document tells us that Alexander Comyn, second Earl of Buchan, who was the King's Justiciary of Scotland, "sat in the Castlesyde of Abirden". This particular site has been identified as that now occupied by the Salvation Army Citadel. This is the grandiose neo-baronial structure, a little reminiscent of Balmoral Castle in style, which now fronts the east end of the square. Designed by James Souttar it dates from 1896.

Though not a trace of it remains today the Castle of Aberdeen played a crucial part in the early history of the burgh. It was occupied by an English garrison during the first Scottish War of Independence, a garrison that must have been detested heartily by the good folk of the burgh, who favoured the cause of their liberator King, Robert the Bruce, whom they had secretly succoured in the darkest days of his struggle against the might of Edward I of England, the Hammer of the Scots.

When Edward I had died and his son reigned in his stead, Bruce's fortunes turned. The new English king sent urgent instructions that his admiral should proceed northward with a fleet "to succour the Castle of Aberdeen". He appears to have been too late. Tradition has it that the burghers of Aberdeen, with the city's motto "Bon-Accord" as their watchword, rose and destroyed both the castle and its garrison. In place of the old castle the citizens later built a chapel which they dedicated to St. Ninian, but the old site was fortified once again in the mid-seventeenth century by General Monck on behalf of Cromwell. A fragment of this Cromwellian bastion still remains on the east side of the Castle Hill.

The oldest structure still visible from the Castlegate is the tower of the Old Tolbooth, the lower and most easterly of the two steeples forming part of the range of public buildings along the north side of the Castlegate. Take a stroll along to the high arched pend leading off the square into Lodge Walk, on which the Old Tolbooth abuts, and you will be able to see it better.

THE OLD TOLBOOTH

It says something for the pride with which the Castlegate, then the largest burgh centre in Scotland, was regarded in the middle ages, that Robert III, King of Scots (1390-1406) in giving approval for the erection of a tolbooth, or burgh jail, on this site explicitly stipulated that it must not be erected in the centre of the forum. That tolbooth served its day and generation and the present Old Tolbooth was built in its place in 1627. The original frontage to Castle Street has now been built over, but by going into Lodge Walk, where the whole height of the original tower is still exposed to view, you can get a very good idea of this sturdy ashlar three-storey square tower with corbelled bartizans. The steeple, with its balustraded parapet and fine lead spire was added in 1629.

From the earliest days the Old Tolbooth was known as the Mids o' Mar (the heart of the province of Mar) on the same principle by which the old Tolbooth of Edinburgh was called the Heart of Midlothian, a title immortalised by Sir Walter Scott's novel. Tower and steeple rise to a height of 120 feet. Originally merely a prison, with grim and tiny cells, the Tolbooth was added to in 1640 by a wing which served as the council chamber, but this was demolished in 1750 to make way for a new Town House, which in its turn made way for the present building.

Though the Tolbooth still has a mellow grandeur suggestive of its great age, it can scarcely compare in charm with the next oldest survival in the Castlegate. Standing now in the centre of the square towards its east end is —

THE MERCAT CROSS

Unquestionably the finest burgh cross surviving in Scotland, it stands like a red sandstone flower to remind us of an era when the "granite city" of today was as yet undreamed of, but when craftsmanship was cherished, and lovely things were carved from softer materials.

Its architect and builder was John Montgomery of Old Rayne, a tiny village in the Garioch, who did the job for Aberdeen Town Council in 1686 at a cost of £100, exclusive of materials, after constructing a model in timber and pasteboard for the approval of the civic fathers. It takes the form of a circular arcade 21 feet in diameter and 18 feet high, with a Corinthian capital rising 16 more feet upwards from the centre of the roof and surmounted by a unicorn of white marble.

It is however in the rich detail of its decoration that the cross is outstanding, containing as it does a unique portrait gallery of the Scottish sovereigns from James I to James VII. The parapet contains twelve compartments. The first two of these, in the middle of the west side, hold sculptured panels of the Royal Arms and the Arms of Aberdeen. Then, moving round to the north, we find King James I, represented by a portrait head with the letters IA and RI on either side. He is followed by James II, James III, James IV, Mary Queen of Scots, James VI, Charles I and II and James VII.

The portraits are by no means negligible approximations. In them one can follow the changes in fashion down the centuries and the later Stuart monarchs, in particular, are allegedly very good likenesses.

The richly engraved capital, the decorative band below the parapet, the fierce looking gargoyles — are they hounds, bears or leopards? — the beauty of the pillars framing the arches, are all works of art.

As McGibbon and Ross put it: "The market cross of Aberdeen is a notable work, both because of its elegant form and because the name of its designer is preserved . . . It does credit to the man who was both its designer and builder".

As we look on this pleasing symbol of civic authority we may remember the tremendous pageant of history that has been enacted in the Castlegate of Aberdeen, both before and after it was erected. It was built

Above:
THE OLD TOLBOOTH
formerly the City's gaol.

Opposite:
THE MERCAT CROSS,
built in 1686.

Baker's

to replace the ancient Flesh Cross of the burgh and stood at first immediately opposite the Old Tolbooth. To the Flesh Cross in 1511 came James IV's young queen, Margaret Tudor, inspiring William Dunbar to write his famous eulogy of the city that begins:

> Blyth Aberdeene, thou beriall of all tounis,
> The lamp of bewtie, bountie and blythness;
> Unto heaven ascendit thy renown is . . .

That the Castlegate was the centre of festivities on this occasion is clear from the poet's words:

> At hir cumming great was the mirth and joy
> For at thair cross abundantlie ran wyne...

Sometimes however, the spectacle was less cheerful. From the Earl Marischal's Lodging, a great house that was demolished to make way for modern Marischal Street, leading from the south side of the Castlegate to the Harbour, Mary Queen of Scots, in 1562, is said to have shed tears on witnessing the beheading of Sir John Gordon by the Maiden, Aberdeen's patent version of the guillotine, as part of the rough justice that followed the Battle of Corrichie.

The Flesh Cross flowed with wine again on June 27, 1597, when the Earls of Huntly and Errol, erstwhile rebels, were received into the Protestant faith. The Cross was covered with tapestry and the earls sat in chairs beside it. At the Cross 'ane litell house' also draped with tapestry, sheltered fourscore young men of the town, musicians in their best finery. A table nearby was laid out with numerous confections, a great number of glasses and 'wyn in grȳt abundance!' After the King's Commissioner had delivered a wand of peace to the earls and received them back to royal favour, the ministers and town council embraced them, toasts were drunk off and sweetmeats scattered on the causeway for all and sundry to scramble for.

In 1745, in the midst of the last Jacobite Rebellion, wine played its part again—this time at the existing Mercat Cross. Here Bonnie Prince Charlie's followers proclaimed the Old Pretender, James VIII, and the luckless Provost of the burgh, James Morison of Elsick, because he remained loyal to George II, and would not drink the Pretender's health, had the wine which he had refused to drink, rudely poured down his shirt-front. This won him the sobriquet of "Provost Positive". It goes without saying that every British sovereign for the past three centuries has also been proclaimed at the Mercat Cross of Aberdeen.

Before we move on to the eighteenth and nineteenth century buildings in the Castlegate, there is one more historic landmark that demands attention. Aberdeen folk know it as "The Mannie" or "The Mannie o' the Green", a leaden sculpture of a nude but modestly loin-clothed figure who stands on top of the rectangular stone fountain on the raised stone platform at the south-west corner of the square. This pleasing pedestrian precinct is called—

THE PLAINSTANES

As we see them today, the Plainstanes are a modern reconstruction. Originally much more extensive, they stood farther east in the centre of the square, and the rectangular fountain topped by the Mannie was an integral part of the burgh's water supply. The fountain was removed from the Castlegate in 1848 and later sited in the Green, that other early market place which lies just south of Union Street and west of Market Street. In 1958, the fountain was dismantled, and with the Mannie put into store where it remained hidden from public view until its replacement in the Castlegate in 1972, once more crowned by the graceful Mannie.

Describing the Plainstanes in their original site fronting the Mercat Cross an early guide book tells us: "Here of old used many of the inhabitants to pass an hour or two in walking before dinner, bracing their nerves in the free air and discussing the politics of the day. This class was named Peripatetics because they so much resembled their ancient prototypes, and like these worthies they are now almost all gathered to their fathers". Round the outer edge of the Plainstanes the fishwomen with their creels, from the nearby fishing hamlets of Findon, Cove and Portlethen, had a prescriptive right to sit and sell their wares.

In the last decade of the eighteenth century, the Plainstanes were haunted by a little lame boy of seven or eight. He was the future Lord Byron, the poet, then living in Broad Street with his mother, and his interest in the Plainstanes was due to his little cousin Mary Duff, who lived in one of the Castlegate houses nearby. He persuaded himself that he was passionately in love with her. "We were the merest children" he wrote later. "I have been attached fifty times since, yet I recollect all we said to each other, all our caresses, her features, my restlessness, my sleeplessness, my tormenting my mother's maid to write for me to her, which she did at last to quiet me. Hearing of her marriage years after was like a thunderstroke".

For those who are interested in period architecture, there are still a number of Georgian houses such as Byron's little sweetheart lived in, surviving in the Castlegate. Opposite the Mercat Cross on the north side, No. 17, the Horseshoe Bar, was built about 1760. It has a fine moulded eaves course and a moulded pend arch on the right leading to Albion Court.

Other eighteenth century houses are to be seen in Castle Terrrace leading south from the east end of the Castlegate, while at the corner of Marischal Street, the block Nos. 51-52 Castle Street and 1-3 Marischal Street was built in 1763. Here by crossing Marischal Street, which will be dealt with later. we can make the transition from the historic to the modern Aberdeen, from the "right little, tight little burgh" of the eighteenth century, closely grouped round the Castlegate and Broad Street, to the expansive Granite City of the nineteenth century based on the mile-long Union Street leading west, and the even longer King Street leading north, both of which were opened up in 1801.

The Bank of Scotland, Nos. 53-54 Castle Street. has historic importance as the first public building of this new age. It was built in

1801 in the grandiose neo-classical style which was to mark this whole epoch, for the Union Bank, to designs by James Burn of Haddington, a three-storey five window structure of granite ashlar with rusticated ground floor of the giant R-doric pilaster order, with tryptich and disc frieze atop the balustrade.

The neo-classical theme is continued in the handsome block which terminates the square west of the Plainstanes, forming Nos. 1 and 2 Castle Street, and Nos. 5-11 Union Street, formerly the Royal Athenaeum Restaurant and originally known as Union Buildings. Although the Union Street portion dates from 1819 the frontage on Castle Street, with its ground floor of six arched windows and arched entrance, with three two-storey windows above flanked by pillars and surmounted by architrave, was not completed until 1822. It was designed by Archibald Simpson (1790-1847) to whom, more than any other man, nineteenth century Aberdeen owes its architectural distinction.

The tall two-storey windows were designed to light the Athenaeum news room of Alexander Brown, a Provost of Aberdeen, who was also a bookseller, and hoped that his stately circulating library would become a rendezvous of all the wealthier citizens. It cost £12,000 but it did not pay, and was sold to one of the newsroom attendants for £5. Then in 1888, it was converted into the Athenaeum Restaurant by James Hay, and despite several changes of ownership since, has been nicknamed by Aberdonians, "Jimmy Hay's" ever since. It was ravaged by fire in 1973 but restored.

The whole of the north side of the Castlegate, from Broad Street to King Street, forms one continuous facade of public buildings, all dating from the nineteenth century with the solitary exception of the Old Tolbooth steeple, already described. But to understand the historical chronology of these buildings, it is better perhaps to begin at the east end with the sector of King Street between the Castlegate and the Queen Street-West North Street-East North Street intersection.

As already mentioned, King Street was opened up in the year 1801. Its first important building was erected in 1816-17 when Archibald Simpson designed St. Andrew's Chapel, now St. Andrew's Episcopal Cathedral. This handsome frontage, recently cleaned, stands on the east side of the Street, a little way north of the Castlegate, and is in Craigleith ashlar in a neo-Perpendicular Gothic style with decorated gable, battlemented and pinnacled, and three noble traceried windows. The porch in front was added by Sir Robert Lorimer in 1911.

The interior of the building is of several periods and of great interest and splendour. The nave is vaulted and has aisles. The chancel was designed by George Edmund Street in 1880. A chancel extension was begun in 1928 and this was followed by the Seabury Memorial restoration, involving complete redecoration and furnishing, and the provision of ciborium and chapel carried out in 1936-43 to the designs of Sir John Ninian Comper. This was the gift of the bishops of the American Episcopal Church. Dedicated in 1948, it commemorates Samuel Seabury, first bishop of the United States, who had been consecrated in Aberdeen in 1748. The American connection is marked by splendid heraldic features.

The remaining part of this eastern side of King Street consists of plain domestic buildings of stately granite ashlar, designed in a uniform style with round headed windows and doorways by John Smith, City Architect of Aberdeen in the 1820's. But if we move across to the west side of the street we can see a remarkable sequence of buildings all with marked neo-Greek characteristics. The earliest of them, No. 29 King Street, is the pillared Medico-Chirurgical Hall built in 1818-20, to plans by Archibald Simpson.

The Aberdeen Medico-Chirurgical Society was founded in 1789 by twelve young doctors "for their mutual improvement in prosecuting their studies by holding weekly meetings at which professional subjects were discussed and discourses delivered and criticised."

Led by James (afterwards Sir James) McGrigor, founder of the Army Medical Corps, these young medicos amassed a valuable medical library, and it was to house this and provide a permanent meeting place that they commissioned Simpson to design for them a medical hall. His bold design of a tetrastyle Ionic portico would have been quite out of proportion standing on its own, but it was arranged with commendable foresight so that when the adjoining spaces on either side came to be feued out for building purposes, the proprietors of the buildings to be erected on these sites should be held bound to make them stand back a little so as to form wings of the main building.

This is exactly what happened. Even although the sites were not built upon for over a decade, the architect for the adjoining blocks happened to be John Smith, the City Architect, and he collaborated with Simpson to complete the entire scheme. The flanking unit on the south side, recessed back from Simpson's portico, became part of the Public Record Office — now the Customs and Excise and Inland Revenue headquarters at 27 King Street. This is a handsome building in its own right, its end bays advanced with anta-pilasters. On the other side of Simpson's portico is now the home of the Aberdeen Children's Theatre, where work goes on under the Education Authority's Speech and Drama Department.

The Children's Theatre in its turn is now directly linked on to the Aberdeen Civic Arts Centre. This building at the King Street - Queen Street corner was erected in 1828-30 as the North Church, and was also designed by John Smith. He planned it in the neo-Greek rectangular giant order with four-column Ionic portico facing Queen Street and gave it a square tower having a cylindrical "tower of winds" top stage — almost a copy of St. Pancras Church in London.

If we now move back towards the Castlegate we can see how another notable architect entered the picture in 1836 when James Gillespie

14

Graham designed Nos. 7-9 King Street. He too was wholly in sympathy with the neo-Greek style of the street and he gave his building an arched ground floor and four R-doric columns in pilasters on the first and second floors.

Finally, the entire group was completed when in 1839 Archibald Simpson designed Nos. 1-5 King Street linking up with the pillared cornerpiece of the Clydesdale Bank (originally the North of Scotland Bank) at the junction of King Street with the Castlegate.

The entire sequence is a masterpiece of integrated classical design.

Archibald Simpson's Clydesdale (or North of Scotland) Bank building marked a turning point in the evolution of the Castlegate. The building he designed is a three-storey structure with cornice on second-floor level, the ground and first floor storeys being channelled with windows in two-storey recesses. The quadrant Corinthian corner portico with its flat platform top is surmounted by a remarkable terra-cotta sculpture designed by James Giles, an artist friend of the architect. Giles, whose dates are 1801-70, was like Simpson himself, a local man. He proved that it was possible to live and even to prosper in Aberdeen as a portrait painter. On the centenary of his death exhibitions of his work were staged in Aberdeen and also in the Ashmolean Museum in Oxford.

Take a look at the gaily painted lady he modelled for the bank portico. At first glance it looks rather like the familiar figure of Britannia. on the back of an old penny. But it is not Britannia. It is Ceres, whom the Greeks knew as Demeter, Goddess of Plenty. She bears a cornucopia of the fruits of the earth — to symbolise the growing prosperity of Aberdeen's farming hinterland in the pushful Victorian Age when the bank was founded. The banking hall interior is particularly fine with Corinthian pilasters and gilt Parthenon frieze. The gold leaf decorations of the ceiling have never needed to be renewed though cleaned innumerable times.

Linking the bank with the Sheriff Courthouse and Municipal Buildings to the west of it in the Castlegate is the arched pend leading to Lodge Walk. The old structures here were the historic New Inn and the plain old Town House swept away in 1868 to make way for the present buildings in which the Town Council Chamber with its glittering chandeliers and civic portraits and the adjoining Town and County Hall, a handsome banqueting hall, are the major features while the Town House tower contains a spectacular circular staircase with vestibule centred by a large marble statue of Queen Victoria. This was the work of Alexander Brodie, a brilliant young Aberdeen sculptor who in 1864 was commissioned to execute a full-length figure of Victoria in Sicilian marble as the "Queen of Scots" to stand at the important corner of Union Street and St. Nicholas Street. Although exquisitely cut the statue did not stand up to the Aberdeen climate and in 1888 was taken indoors to be sited in the lobby of the Town House.

The historic holy-of-holies in the Town House is the Charter Room containing one of the finest collections of civic records anywhere in

Britain, among them the burgh's first charter from King William the Lion (1165-1214) and the famous "Freedom Lands" charter of King Robert the Bruce dated 1319. Among the more modern treasures is the magnificent civic mace presented by Mr. John F. Hall in 1958. Also preserved in the Town House are the handbells used by the burgh's town criers dating from 1697 and 1741.

CONCERT COURT

Behind the Town House and the Sheriff Court lies a little-known street or lane entered from Broad Street and named Concert Court. It takes its name from the weekly concerts held there for a long period in the eighteenth century by the Aberdeen Musical Society who had a hall here. The street was also the site of a little episcopal chapel which was shamefully misused by soldiers of the Duke of Cumberland in 1746, during the campaign that ended in the Battle of Culloden. These old buildings were swept away to make room for the present Town House but in the space that remained on the north side of the lane there was built in 1870-72 Advocates' Hall, the stately home of the Aberdeen Society of Advocates. The site was strategically chosen for the building abuts directly on the flank of the Sheriff Courthouse and a connecting door between the east end of Advocates Hall and the main lobby of the Sheriff Court enables the "men of law" to make a rapid transit from the scene of their pleadings in Court to their social meeting place where morning coffee is a daily rite. Although it has a severely classical exterior, with large round-headed windows and stately pillared and pedimented portico, the interior of Advocates Hall is like a Renaissance palace with long arched corridors and a handsome staircase lit by a window symbolising Justice and rising to a fine galleried library, while the Advocates Hall proper extends northward from the end of the main corridor. Advocates Hall was designed by James Matthews, another prominent architect in Aberdeen, who became Lord Provost of the burgh, and was opened in 1872. The origin of the Society of Advocates in Aberdeen is lost in the mists of antiquity. Early records were destroyed by a fire in 1721 but it is known that advocates were practising in the burgh by the second half of the sixteenth century.

BROAD STREET

Broad Street, where we began our walk-about, and to which we now return, today contains four public buildings—the northward extension of the Town House along the east side of the street from the Castlegate to Queen Street, Greyfriars Church and Marischal College beyond the Queen Street intersection on the same side, and on the other side of the street the massive spread of St. Nicholas House containing local government offices.

"Just a simple office block" was the architect's description of St. Nicholas House completed in 1970 at a cost of £1,897,700. It consists of a long three-storey building extending along Broad Street and down part of Upperkirkgate, centred by a 15-storey tower at right angles to the main spread. By reason of its height this dominates the entire city centre and from the roof walk affords the finest view of Aberdeen in every direction from the Harbour and Aberdeen Bay on the east to the open country beyond the Bridge of Dee on the south-west.

It is the apotheosis of modernity but in the attractive courtyard formed by the extended L-plan of the building and approached by a flight of steps from Broad Street stands in full and fine preservation the oldest domestic dwelling in "new" Aberdeen — Provost Skene's House, now furnished as a period museum open to the public.

The earliest mention of the house on record was in 1545. At that time Scotland was in the throes of the War of the Rough Wooing, Mary Queen of Scots was a three-year-old infant and the Reformation was still 15 years in the future. The house was then a plain L-plan structure. By 1622 the house was owned by a prominent burgess of Aberdeen, Matthew Lumsden. When he became a baillie or magistrate of the burgh he carried out various alterations and left a carving of his coat of arms, impaled with those of his wife, Elizabeth Aberdour, upon a semi-circular pediment in freestone above the east dormer window of the west wing. It is still there today and bears the date 1626.

To Lumsden is attributed the remarkable painted ceiling which covers the timber vault of the long gallery at the top of the west wing. The paintings are in panels on both sides of and in the flat central area of this ceiling, while between the panels are decorative cartouches showing cherubs or angels and such symbols from the Catholic middle ages as the Five Wounds of Christ and the Sacred Monograms. On the western slope is depicted the Annunciation to the Virgin and the Adoration of the Shepherds, while on the east are the Crucifixion and the taking down of Christ from the Cross.

In the flat central part of the roof is a magnificent rendering of the Resurrection, with knights in armour gazing at the Risen Lord. Despite its naivete and distortions the scene has that intense mystical feeling which one associates with a visionary painter like El Greco. It is all very moving, and if Matthew Lumsden had, as we believe anything to do with it, we must revise our ideas of the early Covenanters as stern and rigid Puritans who did not respond to the medieval imagination.

The explanation may be that Matthew employed itinerent craftsmen from the Low Countries who based their work on pre-existing tapestries or engravings of Flemish provenance. It has of course been pointed out that there is nothing in the designs which should seriously offend a Protestant. Yet these paintings remain unique in Scotland because of their religious theme and strongly devotional character. Details of the highly delicate restoration work carried out under the aegis of the Department of the Environment are shown in display cases in the Long Gallery itself.

In 1669 Sir George Skene of Rubislaw, a famous Provost of Aberdeen, acquired the house and so altered it that it took on the external character it retains to this day, adding the main staircase block at the east of the house, inserting the two picturesque round stair turrets and altering the fenestration. Indeed, the house is now so much his, both outside and in that its title of Provost Skene's House could not be more appropriate.

Seventeenth century opulence is apparent in the freestone surround of the main doorway, decorated with carved thistle-and-rose Restoration motifs, surmounted by Sir George's own armorial bearings and the motto 'Gratis a Deo data'. His coat of arms and thistles and roses also appear on the plaster ceilings at the west end of the house. Here there are two rooms which contain the original pine panelling and the decorative plaster in excellent condition.

In the main or east wing the ground floor consists of three barrel-vaulted cellars from the westmost of which a short flight of steps leads to a wine cellar built of brickwork and shelved with flagstones. The main staircase has round arches at the landings and the original seventeenth century timber balustrade, while the large hall on the first floor is paved with Caithness slabs. It has a panelled fireplace flanked by Corinthian columns in mahogany. On the second floor one of the rooms has painted wainscotting of a type that became popular in the eighteenth century. The panels are painted to represent marble or rocky cliffs — the idea being to conceal the pine panelling, which often had conspicuous grain or knots, by something much more sophisticated.

The period furnishing of the house cannot be described in detail here. It has benefited by many fine gifts and loans and by drawing on the city's stores of such treasures it has been possible to recreate the atmosphere of a stately 'town lodging'. There is for example a time-piece by the eighteenth century Aberdeen clockmaker John Gartly, while the National Portrait Gallery agreed to lend a portrait of the Duke of Cumberland, whose sojourn in the house in the early spring of 1746 was a memorable incident in the city's annals.

When he arrived in Aberdeen on February 27, leading his army north towards Culloden it was at first intended to accommodate him in Marischal College, but Provost Skene's mansion, by then divided into two dwellings, one of which belonged to Alexander Thomson of Banchory, was selected as his lodging for the next six weeks.

There were at the time and there have been since two views of his behaviour during his stay. Those with Jacobite sympathies have always tended to paint it in the blackest colours, and there is no doubt truth in the statement that he and his officers "made free with the stocks of provisions, coals, candles, ales and other liquours" but bearing in mind that Jacobites were only too keen to exploit anti-Royalist propaganda against the Duke who afterwards earned the epithet of "Butcher" for his ruthless treatment of his enemies, I am inclined to think that on this occasion he did not act much worse than billeted soldiers of the period were prone to do.

He was in fact made much of during his stay. The town council voted him the Freedom of the City and after he had departed they sent him the burgess ticket in a golden casket. The next royal visitor to Provost Skene's

House was Queen Elizabeth, the Queen Mother, then the Queen Consort of George VI. She came in 1938 at a time when the fate of the old house was undecided, and her advocacy of its claim to restoration proved decisive. It is something more than a coincidence that two decades later Her Majesty also exerted her influence in another conservation controversy, helping to secure the preservation of Provost Ross's House in the Shiprow. But before we turn to this subject the gleaming granite facade of Marischal College on the other side of Broad Street demands our attention.

MARISCHAL COLLEGE

It is part of the greatness of Marischal College that, as a piece of architecture, it inspires passionate advocacy on the one hand, and impassioned denigration on the other. This is because the great Broad Street frontage in elaborate perpendicular gothic is a tour de force of the granite carver's art.

It was designed by A. Marshall Mackenzie and built in 1905 as an extension and completion of the older range of buildings within the quadrangle entered by the massive archway with its colourful frieze of armorial shields. It had just become possible at that period to relieve the severe rectangular lines of granite ashlar with the exuberant fretted detail appropriate to the Gothic period, and so the building came to have what one student versifier called—

> The fourteen hundred golden flags
> Stiff in the windless air,
> The pinnacles and minarets
> Most excellently fair,
> The carven stone, the blazoned pane
> All cunningly bedight . . .

To some purists this is just too much. To them it is a "monster-masterpiece" or "a wedding cake in indigestible grey icing", yet the majority reaction is probably that voiced by George Rowntree Harvey: "I like college and tower most of all when I see them against the placid grey sky, shot with silver, of early evening — the hour and the hue that goes deep into the heart of the Aberdonian who cares for the peculiar beauty of his own city. It is in such an hour that the city and its granite become intimate and revealing".

Marischal College is of course much more than its spectacular Broad Street facade. Layer after layer of sentiment and tradition can be peeled off till one comes to the solitary and original inscription still to be found in a stone let into the archway of the main lobby at the far side of the quadrangle: THAY HAIF SAID, WHAT SAY THEY: LAT YAME SAY. For 257 years it was not merely a "college" but a university complete in all its faculties. It was founded on April 2, 1593 by George, fifth Earl Marischal as a Reformed rival to the pre-existing university of King's College, Old Aberdeen, and the defiant motto referred to the fact that the Earl endowed it with the medieval Greyfriars Monastery as its first home on this site.

Opposite: MARISCHAL COLLEGE (Top) AND PROVOST SKENE'S HOUSE, ABERD

Before we step inside the quadrangle take a second look at the gilded and tinctured frieze of shields above the archway. Reading from left to right they bear the coats of arms of Lord Strathcona, the Burgh of Old Aberdeen, Bishop Elphinstone, the University itself, the Earl Marischal, the City of Aberdeen and Charles Mitchell, donor of the Mitchell Hall and Tower.

The buildings forming the inner three sides of the quadrangle date in the main from 1837 to 1844 and were designed in a simplified Gothic style by Archibald Simpson to replace Old Marischal College (1741-1838) which in its turn had supplanted the "flotsam and jetsam of a building" which was all that remained of the Monastery of the Grey Friars. One of Sir Walter Scott's famous fictional characters, Dugald Dalgetty in "A Legend of Montrose" is depicted as a student here and says Scott "filled a place at the bursar's table, where, if you did not move your jaws as fast as a pair of castanets you were very unlikely to get anything to put between them."

When in 1860, by Act of Parliament, King's and Marischal Colleges were merged into the single University of Aberdeen, the Arts and Divinity faculties went to King's and Medicine, Law and Natural History to Marischal. But soon more room was needed for the new departments of Botany, Chemistry and Pathology and in 1891 the University embarked on a great extension scheme which took 13 years to complete. It entailed the demolition of a long line of old domestic buildings on the east side of Broad Street (in one of which the poet Byron spent his early boyhood) as well as the ancient pre-Reformation Monastery Church of Greyfriars, a beautiful example of Scoto-Gothic in freestone by a distinguished architect Alexander Galloway, dating from the early sixteenth century. It was demolished in 1902. Its noble east window, with superb freestone tracery, was however built into the new granite structure abutting on the south-west range of Marischal College that houses the Greyfriars Church of today.

The first changes were at the east side of the quadrangle where benefactions by Charles Mitchell and his son made possible the erection of the Mitchell Hall—where graduation ceremonies have ever since been held—and the raising of Archibald Simpson's central tower to a height of 235 feet as the Mitchell Tower. Other features here are the Picture Gallery, and the Anthropological Museum—with a particularly fine collection of treasures from all over the world.

The extensions as a whole were opened by Edward VII and Queen Alexandra on September 27, 1906. The Chancellor, Lord Strathcona, gave on the evening of the great day a dinner to over 2,400 guests which has gone down in history as the most lavish feast in all Aberdeen's annals.

On right of the entrance to the quadrangle is situated the University Court Room with its splendid heraldic ceiling where the coats of arms include those of Edward VII, Bishop Elphinstone, Earl Marischal, three Chancellors, three Lord Provosts, four Principals and the Mitchell and Carnegie families.

Since 1906 more than three-quarters of the departments originally housed in Marischal College have moved to new homes of their own. Internal conversion has been extensive. In 1966 the old Gymnasium was converted into a library housing 30,000 volumes while the high ceiling (17½ ft.) in most of the rooms in the spacious Edwardian layout have allowed the construction of mezzanine floors virtually doubling the usefulness of the accommodation.

The Students Union, formerly housed inside the College now has its own building at the corner of Upperkirkgate and Gallowgate at the north end of Broad Street.

SHIPROW AND MARISCHAL STREET

To complete our walk around the Castlegate and its immediate environs we now retrace our steps to the south end of Broad Street and, crossing the east end of Union Street by a handy pedestrian crossing, turn down a pedestrian way into Shiprow, the sloping and curving street leading down to the Harbour. Shiprow is also linked to Castlegate and the Plainstanes by a short street behind Union Buildings called Exchequer Row. It takes its name from the exchequer or mint set up in Aberdeen at the end of the twelfth century by King William the Lion.

Although the Shiprow was probably more ancient than the Castlegate itself, forming the link between it and a still earlier settlement at the mouth of the Denburn, it is notable today for one building only. On the right or west side of the brae, opposite a twentieth century supermarket and multi-storey car park, is Provost Ross's House, the second oldest domestic building in the city centre.

The house originally built in 1593 consisted of a rectangular main block with two projecting towers, front and back, both of which are finished with simple well-proportioned gables. Along with the two adjoining houses, Nos. 48 and 50 Shiprow it was rescued from a state of near collapse and ruin and restored after a national campaign by preservationists in 1952, to which Queen Elizabeth, the Queen Mother, ient her powerful advocacy.

By agreement with the National Trust for Scotland Provost Ross's House will contain Aberdeen's maritime museum.

Ross's House is thought to have been built by Andrew Jamesone (a prominent Aberdeen mason who was the father of George Jemesone, Scotland's first notable portrait painter) to the orders of Robert Watson, a

wright or joiner, and his wife Margaret Collie, whose initials have been found on the spur stones. A century later John Ross of Arnage, a famous Provost of Aberdeen, acquired the house and altered it, inserting a new front door on the east front—so that he could see from his doorstep his own trading ships in the Harbour.

> The Provost stood at the door of his house
> And he counted his ships on the tide,
> And he sailed on a barque to the Low Countrie,
> And in Amsterdam he died.
>
> But the house that he bought and plenished so fine
> Lived on when he was dead,
> And MacGibbon and Ross admired its line,
> "In some respects unique," they said
> And that was all very fine.
>
> But a graceless age took little care
> Of the house on the Shiprow Brae;
> And what with its years and its wear and tear
> It fell on an evil day.

It was certainly touch and go whether the old house would be pulled down or rehabilitated. The reconstruction of the building was carried out to plans by A. G. R. Mackenzie, architect, son of the designer of the Marischal College extension. There are interesting old stone carvings within the house and the Arms of Provost Ross have been placed in the moulded recess on the north wall of the front tower. The adjoining houses, Nos. 48 and 50 Shiprow date from 1710.

To the lover of Georgian architecture, Marischal Street, the long straight street running down to the Harbour from the centre of the Castlegate, to the east of the Shiprow, is of special interest as it is the only complete Georgian street left in the city.

A page or two back mention was made of the great old mansion known as the Earl Marischal's Lodging and its association with Mary Queen of Scots. It was here in 1716 that the disheartened chiefs of the Jacobite army in retreat after the Battle of Sheriffmuir had gathered to learn that their "king", James the Seventh, the Old Pretender, had deserted the sinking ship and slipped out of the country on a vessel from Montrose. The Tenth Earl Marischal later followed his master to the continent and, after a famous career there under Frederick the Great of Prussia, was pardoned for his part in the Rising, by George III.

After a brief return to Scotland he chose to go back to Berlin, where his services were much in demand, and the old mansion was deserted and unused. So in 1763 the magistrates of Aberdeen negotiated with him "the purchase of his Lordship's lodging . . . for the opening up of a passage from the Castlegate of the burgh to the Shore and erecting a street there."

Standing on the corner of Castle Street and King Street, site of the historic New Inn, the Clydesdale Bank's Chief Aberdeen office is one of the finest examples of granite masonry anywhere in the world. With its terra cotta statue of Ceres, the Goddess of plenty overlooking the Castlegate, it was designed in 1842 for the North of Scotland Banking Company by Archibald Simpson.

Today, over 100 years later, the Clydesdale Bank is still providing the people of Aberdeen with a complete banking service, a service tailored to meet the needs of our individual customers.

Find out how many helpful financial services we do provide; call at your local Branch for a booklet or write or phone for an appointment with the Manager — YOU DON'T HAVE TO BE A CUSTOMER.

Clydesdale Bank

CHIEF ABERDEEN OFFICE:
5 CASTLE STREET

The deal was completed on Whitsunday 1764, the Treasurer paying the Earl Marischal £803 3s 4d as the price of the building and in 1766 the council decided to make the new street 40 feet wide. It was the first street in Aberdeen paved with squared granite setts and the houses themselves were of granite ashlar, uniformly of three stories and an attic high and with three-window frontages. The street was being built when Boswell and Johnson visited Aberdeen in 1773. No doubt it was Marischal Street that Johnson had in mind when he remarked in his "Journey to the Western Isles" — "The houses are large and lofty . . . They build almost wholly with granite used in the new pavement of the streets of London, which is well known not to want hardness, yet they shape it easily. It is beautiful and must be very lasting".

Midway on its way from Castlegate to the harbour the new street had to cross over low-level Virginia Street. It did so by means of a very solid fly-over bridge, called Bannerman's Bridge after the mason Alexander Bannerman who built it for a little over £600. Unfortunately this sturdy old structure was doomed in 1973 when a public inquiry decided it would have to be replaced by a wider bridge so that Aberdeen's Inner Ring Road might pass under it.

In its early days Marischal Street was a fashionable residential quarter. Two well-known artists were born in it. The first was Andrew Robertson, sometimes called the "father of miniature painting" and the second was William Dyce, R.A., a promoter of the Pre-Raphaelite movement. The street has many pleasing details such as pillared and fanlighted doorways.

Although now completely out of character with the rest of the street there is historical interest in Marischal Street's one ecclesiastical building — on the west side near the harbour end. Begun in 1788 this was the Theatre Royal, Aberdeen's home of legitimate drama for 78 years — from 1794 to 1872. It then became the Trinity Parish Church, being rebuilt in the Gothic revival style which it still displays today as the Elim Gospel Church. Behind it in Theatre Lane are the old theatre dressing rooms, now in use as a joinery workshop.

Although the new and widened Inner Ring Road must inevitably make some inroads on Marischal Street's solid Georgian uniformity it is part of the city's Conservation Area No. 2 and every affort will be made to retain its architectural character.

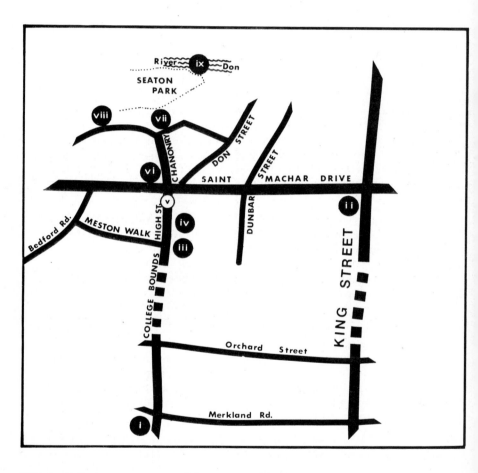

This Map covers Chapter II (pages 29-47)

THE ITEMS OF INTEREST DO NOT NECESSARILY FOLLOW THE EDITORIAL ORDER.

I	St. Margaret's Convent	VI	Cruickshank Botanic Gardens
II	College of Agriculture	VII	St. Machar's Cathedral
III	King's College	VIII	Wallace Tower
IV	Wrights' & Coopers' Place	IX	Brig O' Balgownie
V	Old Aberdeen Town House		

CHAPTER II — OLD ABERDEEN

No one who visits Aberdeen can or should attempt to escape the spell of Old Aberdeen — the Aulton as it is affectionately called. If you are using public transport the simplest way to get there is by the Students' Bus, No. 20, which starts from Littlejohn Street near its junction with Gallowgate directly opposite the northern flank of Marischal College. If you go by car the simplest way is perhaps to travel north along King Street till you reach the major intersection of St. Machar Drive on the left hand side where under the shadow of the massive block of the new College of Agriculture you turn left to enter the Aulton at its central point, where the Old Aberdeen Town House, occupying an island site, stands with its back to the busy traffic artery and faces High Street.

Owing to a restricted access system there is no direct entry from St. Machar Drive to High Street for cars. The way in for them is by Elphinstone Road, a little to the west, where an entirely new street has been formed, or by Dunbar Street, a short distance to the east, while at the southern end of the University Precinct the approach is by Regent Walk, which connects King Street with College Bounds.

Either way you will find that the High Street, ancient, tree shaded, redolent of centuries of peaceful development, is the fulcrum and focus of the carefully preserved university village. A famous Principal of the University of Aberdeen, Sir Thomas Taylor, gave in the years just following the end of World War II, a memorable pledge about the Aulton in these words: "The University Court has all along considered that it was of the essence of any plan of development that the architecture, character and demographic composition of what is essentially a village community should be preserved".

Aberdeen Corporation felt the same way about it, which is why Old Aberdeen was later designated as Aberdeen's Conservation Area No. 1 and why Town as well as Gown has played a major part in safeguarding the atmosphere of the Aulton. This is why, despite the twentieth century architecture with which it is now so closely environed — the high rise flats of Tillydrone and Seaton, the rather futuristic departmental teaching blocks of the University, the student halls of residence — Old Aberdeen is still 'old' in fact as well as in name. It consists of what is really a single line of street: College Bounds, High Street and Don Street (all part of the ancient highway from Aberdeen to the north) and Chanonry, a loop to the west so called because in the middle ages it contained the 'manses' of the Canons of the Cathedral of St. Machar, which terminates the Aulton on the north.

Today this medieval village contains a mixture of dwellings of every century from the sixteenth to the twentieth, in addition to some structures that are still older, but the important thing is that all retain the village atmosphere and a unity of character, a character they were given in the

Left: POWIS LODGE GATEWAY which now leads to Crombie Hall

Below: OLD ABERDEEN HIGH STREET and TOWN HOUSE

days when Old Aberdeen was an independent burgh quite distinct from 'new' Aberdeen and contained besides the university students and the professors and cathedral clergy a 'mixed' community of small traders. The preservation of this mixed community was made possible by the fact that nearly all the houses were owned by the university, who were assisted in a scheme of restoration by grants from the Lady MacRobert General Trust. What they have been able to do we shall see as we make our tour.

And here we shall fall back on the No. 20 bus which after all provides the logical approach to the riches of the Aulton. It takes its way from the 'new' town by Littlejohn Street and East North Street, now part of the city's Inner Ring Road, to the big roundabout at Mounthooly overlooked by the soaring Gallowgate High Flats, and from that point onwards by way of Mounthooly, King's Crescent and Spital along a route familiar to generations of students, traversing the old high road northwards, as 'the Spital Brae'. There are some interesting old houses on the left of this route and among them an interesting essay in granite, St. Margaret's Convent, designed by Sir Ninian Comper and built in 1898.

As we reach the crown of the hill at the top of the Spital brae we have an interesting example of the way in which the existence of the Old Aberdeen conservation area has influenced modern planners. The east side of the street was recently rebuilt between Orchard Street and Merkland Road and the 56 new council houses in this scheme have been given projecting gables, stair towers and a touch of corbelling to attain a strikingly traditional look as a foretaste of the Aulton proper. The housing complex at the top of the hill is called St. Peter's Gate and as we begin to descend on the other side and pass the delightful paved and flagged court (another new council scheme) at Spital Walk we enter Old Aberdeen proper with No. 1 College Bounds.

Here we step right into the eighteenth century, for this typical two storey three window ashlar house with its gay red pantiles belongs to that period. The next two houses on that side of the street — the west — belong to a later date but No. 7 is another eighteenth century house, also pantiled and partly of ashlar and partly of rubble construction. At No. 19 College Bounds we come to one of those remarkable stretches of stout old walling, which, apart from the college and the cathedral and Chaplain's Court are virtually the oldest works of man's hand surviving in the Aulton. This one dates from the early sixteenth century.

It is rubble-built and contains a built-up moulded and segmented archway surmounted by Bishop Elphinstone's coat of arms. It is thought that this archway originally led to the now vanished Snow Kirk, the burgh church of the Aulton. Behind the wall today lie the Humanity Manse, originally the home of the Latin professors, the university computer building and the Johnston Hall of Residence. It is by a little gated path leading south from the approach to Johnston Hall that one now arrives at the venerable Snow Kirkyard itself — today only a tiny enclave walled in and kept apart from the profusion of twentieth century buildings with which it is surrounded. It has only one stone of special interest, a great armorial slab containing the date 1669 and the name of a famous Aberdeen magnate, Gilbert Menzies of Pitfodels, but the story of how the old burgh kirk of the Aulton came to have such an exotic name never fails to charm.

The Church of St. Mary ad Nives was founded by Bishop Elphinstone in virtue of a Bull from Pope Alexander VI dated March 18, 1497, two years after the founding of King's College itself. In the Aberdeen Breviary which he wrote the good bishop showed his special interest in the legend attaching to the origin of S. Maria Maggiore in Rome, the second church in Christendom. The story goes that in the time of Pope Liberius, John, a Roman patrician and his wife, being childless, wished to spend their fortune in honour of the Virgin. While the Pope was considering this, he had a dream in which St. Mary appeared and signified to him that she wished to have a church dedicated to her on the Esquiline Hill. The site, she said would be marked out by snow.

Next day, although the month was August, and the heat in Rome intense, it was found that snow had fallen and S. Maria Maggiore was duly erected on the site. Bishop Elphinstone, for his part, fixed the festival of St. Mary ad Nives in August and told the story of the miracle in six sections.

Most of the remaining houses in College Bounds belong to the early nineteenth century but at the foot of the gradual descent we come to an architectural climax marked on the east side by King's College itself and on the west by the oriental effloresence of Powis Lodge Gate with its minarets and arch, now spanning the driveway to the Crombie Hall of Residence.

KING'S COLLEGE

King's College in its gracious and mellow freestone is a unified complex of buildings in Scottish Gothic begun in 1500 and with sections not completed until the latter half of the nineteenth century. But the whole composition is still and always will be dominated by the Crown and Tower and the lovely Chapel begun in the first year of the sixteenth century when the Founder, Bishop Elphinstone (1431-1514) was still alive to further the work.

William Elphinstone, statesman and Chancellor of Scotland, obtained the Foundation Bull of the University of Aberdeen, originally the College of St. Mary, issued by Pope Alexander IV, the Borgia Pope, dated February 10, 1494. He it was who induced King James IV of Scotland to petition the Pontiff to the effect that in the northern parts of his kingdom there were "men who were rude, ignorant of letters and almost barbarous" and so incapable of the ministry of the church.

The opening words of the Papal Bull declare that "among the other blessings which mortal man is able to obtain in this fleeting life, it deserves to be reckoned not the least that by earnest study he may win the pearl of knowledge, which shows the way to living well and happily . . . leads to a clear understanding of the secrets of the universe . . . and raises to eminence those born in the lowest estate".

This year of 1494 was something of an **annus mirabilus**, for after the Papal Bull had been received King James IV by charter dated December 26 created "the Cathedral city of Ald Aberdeen a true and free burgh of barony for ever" so that from this point on all three elements in Old Aberdeen were already in being — the church, the university and the burgh.

For four hundred years the pride of Old Aberdeen in its university has been expressed in a visible symbol, the great imperial crown which tops the tower of King's College. Poets and versifiers by the score have acclaimed the Crown of King's. An early chronicler described it as "a most curious and statelie work of hewin and corned stones, representing to the view of all beholders a brave pourtrait of the royal diademe" while at the end of last century Rachel Annand Taylor declared her love for it in these lines:

What marvellous mad hopes were cherished
    In Aberdeen!
Oh, that's a city to be born in.
The pure air kindles you, and witty
Your mind goes dancing. To learn scorn in
Oh, that's a city!
Under the Crown that dreams of Flodden
And Borgia, in a scarlet gown
Youth lightly treads where youth has trodden
Under the Crown.

The reference to Borgia, the Pope of the Foundation Bull, you will already understand. The reference to Flodden is a reminder that the king who shared in the founding, James IV, died in that battle with the flower of his Scottish army in the year 1513, while the good Bishop Elphinstone, the Founder himself, died in the following year — it is said of a broken heart. His tomb covered by a great black slab lay for centuries in the Chapel which he had built between 1500 and 1504 (a date marked on the building). But in this century many of the former students who had worn the "scarlet gown" in King's College joined together and commissioned a magnificent tomb and a sarcophagus in which the effigy of the Good Bishop is upheld by the figures of the 7 Virtues. These bronze figures were cast in Venice in 1914 and during the years of World War I lay under the waters of the Grand Canal, but in time they reached Aberdeen and today stand nobly on the tomb in its present-day position on the lawn in front of the Chapel.

The Crown of King's — whose only equal in Scotland is the crown of Edinburgh's High Kirk of St. Giles — has not been without vicissitudes. It was blown down in a storm in the year 1633 but replaced in the following year with Renaissance ornamentation designed by Dr. William Gordon, Professor of Medicine, the mason being George Thomson.

The Chapel, aisleless, in ashlar freestone, having six bays and three-sided apse, with stout buttresses and large traceried windows at north side and in apse, retains the arrangements and fittings of a medieval collegiate church in a better state of preservation than any other example in the British Isles. It has a ribbed arched wooden ceiling and its richly carved oaken rood screen and stalls have survived almost complete and are by far the finest example remaining of medieval Scottish ecclesiastical woodwork. No wonder that it is the dream and the privilege of great numbers of graduates to be married in this holy of holies.

If you pass through the archway and take a look round the King's College quadrangle, noting the brightly tinctured coats of arms on the outside wall of the Chapel, there are two more points of special interest. In the angle at the south-east corner of the Chapel is the Cromwell Tower, a rather stark and featureless rectangle. Begun in 1658 to provide living accommodation for students — the residential hostel of its day — it is an instance of the 'castle complex' which is one of the odd architectural themes rather common in Aberdeen. Local builders were so obsessed by the medieval castle that almost any public building they conceived down to the end of the seventeenth century was apt to take a castellated form. So here we have "a huge and massive square tower, six storeys high, with a flat roof and an open parapet, for all the world like a Norman keep".

From this relic of the Commonwealth we turn to a much handsomer structure, the University Library. Fronted by a sculptured unicorn — symbol of immaculate virtue and divine wisdom — it was commenced in 1870 and completed in 1885 and occupies the site of the ancient college kitchen, extending over 200 feet eastwards. It takes the form of a long and lofty hall with double transepts. As Sir Robert Rait puts it: "The whole effect is impressive. No library in Scotland is so magnificently housed". To the north of the old Quadrangle is the stately Elphinstone Hall, added in 1931 to celebrate the quincentenary of Bishop Elphinstone's birth.

Before we continue eastward into High Street a backward glance is called for to the second last house on the west side of College Bounds (Nos. 51 and 51½). This is Powis Lodge built in 1697, though re-modelled in 1711 and again in 1829. The builder of the house was Alexander Fraser, Regent, Professor of Greek, and Sub-principal of King's College, who at the end of the seventeenth century acquired twelve roods of land "waste, watery and almost uninhabitable" running along the west side of College Bounds and these twelve roods became the nucleus of a large estate to which he gave the name Powis (from the Gaelic "the pool of fishes"). In 1711 the house was extended by a wing to the west, embellished in 1829 with a bow window and further added to in 1834 by the addition of a minaret.

Rock. Ho.
Nursery

34

This part of Powis Lodge can be seen by passing through the spectacular towered gateway to the south leading from College Bounds to Crombie Hall (already mentioned), built in 1960 as the first mixed hostel for students in Britain. Both the gateway with its centre arch flanked by elaborate minarets, and the minaret of Powis Lodge, were designed by a young architect named Alexander Fraser for John Leslie, a young laird of Powis who had become enamoured of the romantic Turkish poetical romances of the poet Byron, and wished to leave some traces of the Byronic cult behind him. When he had the minaretted gates built in 1834, Leslie removed from the original Powis Lodge an inset panel dating from 1697 and bearing the arms of Sub-principal Alexander Fraser, and built it into the inside of the arch between the minarets — thus in a strange way linking the **first** Alexander Fraser with his architect namesake of 137 years later! A little to the south-west of the minaretted gateway is the house called Powis Gate, now the University Department of Music, but at one time the home of J. G. Burnett of Powis who in 1936 sold the remainder of the estate to Aberdeen Corporation, who built upon it the housing development now embracing Bedford Avenue, Powis Crescent and Circle and Powis Academy.

Turning northward again, with a passing glance at the handsome professor's 'manse' which looks out across a green lawn to King's College, we now cross Meston Walk and enter High Street. The pleasant small

houses on the west side date from the late eighteenth and early nineteenth century while on the right, beyond Elphinstone Hall, is New King's, the home of the University Department of English Literature. Beyond that again is the Old Brewery (now part of King's College) separated by three older houses from the modern block of the Taylor Building (1962), named after Principal Sir Thomas Taylor and housing appropriately, for he was himself a man of law, the Faculty of Law and the Department of Extra-Mural Studies.

Several lanes and short streets lead off the High Street on either side, among them Duncan's Place and Douglas Place on the west, with old-world pantiled houses, but most notable are Grant's Place and Wright's and Cooper's Place on the east — scene of a most notable exercise in restoration, for which the university received the special commendation of the Aberdeen Civic Society.

Nos. 1 to 3 Grant's Place, a row of single-storey rubble-built pantiled cottages dating back to 1732, finely restored in 1965, give a good idea of what most of the dwellings in the Aulton must have looked like in the late seventeenth and early eighteenth centuries. They were little more than but-and-bens but still retaining a moving period quality.

Immediately to the north of this row is the charming Wright's and Cooper's Place with paved pedestrian precinct, small flower-gardens and a modern pond and metal-sculptured sundial, designed to set off what is undoubtedly the showpiece of Old Aberdeen restorations. The houses here are all of two storeys, reflecting the greater urbanity and sophistication of the Aulton burgesses as the eighteenth century advanced. Nos. 3-5 is a handsome two-storey, four-window block, rendered and pantiled, with a bay window added. No. 4, also pantiled and rubble built dates from the early nineteenth century. Nos. 5-5A with its three-window front is slated and has been much rebuilt.

Immediately opposite Wright's and Cooper's Place on the west side of High Street in an open paved courtyard backed by the nineteenth century St. Mary's Church (now converted for use as a university department) is the burgh of Old Aberdeen's ancient Mercat Cross, the shaft of which bears the insignia of the Virgin Mary.

From this point northwards the High Street presents a succession of period houses all handsomely restored. No. 96 with its moulded doorway and two dormers dates from 1623 while Nos. 100, 104 and No. 106 all date from the early eighteenth century. No. 108 is dated 1751. The climax is reached with the Old Aberdeen Town House itself on its island site facing down the middle of the street. It is undoubtedly Aberdeen's most charming Georgian building, with its three storeys each with three windows, the centre bay projecting and with a pediment under the square clock stage and cupola. There seems to be some doubt as to the actual date of the building. First built in 1721 it was either entirely rebuilt or modified in 1788 to a plan prepared by the architect George Jaffray.

Certainly the coat of arms of the burgh of Old Aberdeen above the door had been displayed on the older building. It shows the Lilies of the Aulton: "Azure, a boughpot or, charged with three salmon in fret proper, and containing as many lilies of the garden, the dexter in bud, the centre in full bloom, the sinister half-blown, also proper, flowered argent".

The azure or light blue ground symbolises heaven and the immaculate conception, the white lilies indicate virginity and the fish the Holy Trinity. The progression from bud to withering flower is a pageant of growth and decay. Across the way in Don Street (No. 55 to be exact) is a three-storey eighteenth century house with a two-storey wing called the Dower House, about which a fragrant story is told.

"It is built, as some say" writes Ella Hill Burton "on the site of the old Treasurer's House of the Cathedral, who had among other duties that of keeping the altars decked for service. In its old garden were found numberless roots of the French or Aulton Lily, the fleur-de-lys, whose pure and virginal flowers blossomed where more modish blossoms were desired, and these old altar decorations were dug out with difficulty by the gardener's spade. "The grass withereth, the flower fadeth . . ." But the Lilies of the Aulton are with us still.

Across St. Machar Drive, on the other side of the Old Town House, Don Street leads on to the north while to the west of it the Chanonry pursues its stately, tree-lined way to the Cathedral. Before we consider these it is worth remembering that in the former Market Lands of Old Aberdeen lying west of the High Street are the twentieth century buildings of several university departments: the massive five-storey Chemistry Block, opened in 1952 and since extended, the futuristic-looking Science Library, the Department of Natural Philosophy with its mushroom-shaped vestibule and the University Refectory facing on St. Machar Drive and looking across it to the Botany Department on the other side.

The whole area on the east side of High Street, the rectangle bounded by High Street, St. Machar Drive, King Street and Regent Walk, long occupied by the University playing fields, has recently been developed in a way that deserves study as an example of sensitive design. In addition to New Kings and the Taylor Building, already mentioned, this contains the Administrative Building in Regent Walk, the Audio-Visual Aids Centre, the Lecture Hall, the Study Block, the Arts Lecture Theatre, the massive School of Agriculture and the most attractive of them all, the Edward Wright Building, a general purposes arts block flanking the east side of Dunbar Street. This has been shaped on a curve to follow the old street pattern and the walling that borders a strip of lawn and trees has been carried out in Hopeman stone which has a warm, mellow look.

On the east side of Don Street at its junction with St. Machar Drive is a pleasantly modest scheme of old peoples' houses on the courtyard plan called Bede House Court. It takes this name from the Bede House, Nos. 20 and 22 Don Street. This characterful old building with a projecting tower and a corbelled stair turret was built in 1676 and used at one time to

That'll teach you to show off in company.

house the 'bedesmen' from a still earlier structure called Dunbar's Hospital founded by Bishop Gavin Dunbar and provided with a charter signed by King James V in 1536. Although they no longer live in the Bede House, eight old men of Old Aberdeen still benefit from the bishop's benefaction. They are the official Bedesmen of the Aulton and receive a monthly pension and — in virtue of a very ancient privilege — 3½ pounds' weight of salmon (from the heritors of the Cruives of Don and Nether Don fishings) twice a year. Acquired and restored by Aberdeen Corporation the Bede House is now let out in flats to town council tenants.

Houses on both sides of Don Street, some picturesquely pantiled, have shared in the general restoration while between Don Street and Dunbar Street, to the east of it, runs Clark's Lane with its three attractive small cottages now finely restored, while the lane is charmingly paved and cobbled. So far the domestic dwellings we have been looking at have been small and intimate—part of the crowded common life of an old Scottish burgh. The Chanonry is rather different. Here the houses are large and detached, the stately homes of the university professors.

THE CHANONRY

One of the first things we are conscious of in the Chanonry is the massive boundary wall on the west side and extending along St. Machar Drive to enclose the Botany Department and the Cruickshank Botanic Gardens. This again is a relic of ancient days and was originally rubble-built and coped in the seventeenth century. The gardens themselves, occupying what was once the playing field of the Gymnasium, a famous but now vanished private school, are open to the public and contain many curious and interesting plants.

The big houses on both sides of the street mostly belong to the eighteenth or early nineteenth century, though there are one or two more modern structures, like No. 3 on the east side, which dates from 1937 but was consciously designed in the eighteenth century manner by the late Dr. William Kelly, a noted antiquarian architect. At No. 9 (west side) we come to Mitchell's Hospital, a charming single storey complex on the H-plan of coursed rubble with centre gable and bellcote and with a sundial in the court. This was built in 1801 as an early experiment in old folks' homes "to clothe and maintain five widows and five unmarried daughters of Merchant and Trade Burgesses of Old Aberdeen".

No. 13 Chanonry, on the east side, almost opposite the Marriage Porch and main gateway of St. Machar's Cathedral, the soaring West Front, of which now towers up into view, is Chanonry Lodge, the official home of the Principal of the University. Built in the late eighteenth century and remodelled in 1830 it consists of a two-storey centre block with mansard roof and H-plan pedimented wings.

The houses on this side of the Chanonry, where it takes a right-angle turn to the east and leads back to Don Street, are screened by another of the characteristic massive coped boundary walls. This one of stone and brickwork dates from 1719. The boundary wall at No. 16, with its moulded gateway, is even older, dating from the seventeenth century.

Finally on what is now the north side of Chanonry, at No. 20, is Chaplain's Court, now the home of the Secretary of the University, and a building of very special interest as it contains part of the oldest surviving building in either Old or New Aberdeen. As it stands today it is mainly seventeenth century or later, but includes relics of the original Chaplain's Court of the early sixteenth century. To confirm this for yourself look out for the moulded pend arch surmounted with the arms of Bishop Gavin Dunbar, appointed to the See of Aberdeen in 1518. They consist of a shield with three rectangular cushions surmounted with a bishop's mitre.

The building of today is of three storeys part rubble, part ashlar with coped chimneys and crowsteps, and part-pantiled wings.

It was in 1519 that Bishop Dunbar built the original Chaplain's Court at the south end of the bishop's garden. It enclosed a large square court and had a tower at each of the four corners. It contained accommodation for twenty vicars or chaplains who performed the common service of the cathedral.

ST. MACHAR'S CATHEDRAL

Having explored the Chanonry it is now time to survey the Cathedral itself. Move back please to the main gateway, or better still to the corner of the churchyard in front of the two great western towers, for these are the special glory of the exterior. St. Machar's Cathedral, the Cathedral of Aberdeen, is one of the finest examples of a fortified church surviving in western Europe. This blatantly defensive aspect is due to the fact during the fourteenth and fifteenth centuries the burgh of Aberdeen was a dangerous place to live in. On the one side it was likely to be attacked by the English landing from the sea, on the other side by the Celtic Highlanders descending from the mountains. This is why, when the cathedral was rebuilt between 1424 and 1440 the aisles and nave were crested with embattled parapets, while the two western towers have great machiolated warheads in the manner of a contemporary castle.

Machiolations are the spaces between the corbels supporting a parapet, specially designed for dropping 'solids or liquids' — usually boiling lead — on an attacking enemy. Look up at the parapets of these

great western towers (now surmounted by additional steeples and spires) and you will see these machiolations. They are a perpetual reminder of the turbulent conditions under which St. Machar's Cathedral came into being.

It was by no means the first structure on the site. The cathedral stands on a high grassy platform overlooking, to the north, what is now Seaton Park in the haughland or river meadow of the Don, precisely at the point where, in a wide meander, it takes a shape roughly resembling that of a shepherd's crook. This was the site to which, according to hallowed tradition, St. Machar was directed in the sixth century and there he founded his church. The generally accepted date of the foundation is 580 AD.

In the twelfth century King David I of Scotland transferred a bishop's See from Mortlach in Banffshire to Old Aberdeen, then a village 'of four ploughs' (known as the Kirktown of Seaton). Of the Norman cathedral then built, nothing now survives but a single carved stone preserved in the charter room above the vestry. It fell into ruin and a new cathedral was commenced in 1357. It was never really completed, for by the time of the Reformation 200 years later the new choir was not yet finished. What we have today, therefore, is the nave, with parts of the ruined transepts. It is aisled, and the two most easterly pillars (fourteenth century) are of sandstone, but the greater part of the building is of granite.

This fact in itself is something very extraordinary, for although Aberdeen is known as 'the Granite City' this speciality did not begin, generally speaking, to be taken seriously until the mid-eighteenth century. In the middle ages the masons of the North-east worked only with freestone, which was quarried at a few places in Aberdeenshire and Kincardine but in the main imported by sea from Covesea in Moray. But in the years from 1420 to 1440 the supply of freestone suddenly dried up and for twenty years throughout a period which historians now call 'the Granite Interregnum' the use of granite was the only alternative.

It so happened that this period coincided with the building of these great western towers of St. Machar's. In this period a local master mason, working for Bishop Henry de Lichtoun, apparently as Fenton Wyness has put it, "entirely ignorant of orthodox ecclesiastical tradition, massed his granite blocks as if for defence, simplified mouldings into rough rounds and channels, and contemptuous of any refinements, produced a great west window of seven lights, thus creating something original and quite different from anything done before or since". It is agreed today that the West Front is the finest feature of the cathedral and has "a wonderful symmetry, strength and dignity". The west doorway has in its centre a niche which formerly contained a statuette, possibly that of 'Our Lady of Aberdeen', now in the Church of Finistre in Brussels.

Originally the western towers were topped by castle-like cap-houses, but in the following century Bishop Gavin Dunbar, who did so much in other ways to soften the asperities of his episcopal inheritance, had them replaced by spires of sandstone. For centuries these "twin spires" of St. Machar's were, with the Crown of King's College, the sole landmarks visible from afar above the skyline of Old Aberdeen. Today both are dwarfed by surrounding skyscrapers and other massive modern blocks.

Bishop Henry de Lichtoun died in 1441 and his successor, Bishop Ingram Lindsay roofed the nave of the Cathedral, ceiled it with red fir and covered it with slate. But the final glory of the interior was also due to Bishop Dunbar who, about 1520, installed the magnificent heraldic ceiling consisting of a series of 48 coats of arms, arranged in three parallel lines of 16. Those on the south side represent the kings and nobles of Scotland, the centre row is devoted to the reigning Pope, and Archbishops and Bishops of Scotland while the north row represents the kings of Europe. At the west end of each row are local coats of arms: Aberdeen on the south, King's College in the centre and Old Aberdeen on the north.

Besides notable examples of stained glass (including three windows in the south aisle by Dr. Douglas Strachan) the font is an interesting work of art with sculpture by Hew Lorimer. The front depicts St. Machar baptising converts in the River Don while on the rim are carved words from the 47th Paraphrase, "When to the sacred font we came" intermingled with waves and the little fishes, the **pisciculi** of early Christian symbolism.

The cathedral organ, built by Willis in 1890, with 40 speaking stops controlling 2710 pipes, was recently rebuilt at a cost of £18,000 with the idea of making it more suitable for the classical age of organ music.

SEATON PARK

From the cathedral there are alternative ways in which to approach the renowned Brig o' Balgownie or Old Bridge of Don, one of Aberdeen's greatest monuments of the middle ages.

One may either return to King Street and continue north, crossing the new Bridge of Don and reach the Brig via Balgownie Road and Cot Town, or cross Seaton Park which is entered by a gate from Tillydrone Road to the west of the Cathedral.

By taking the latter route one may see by the way two interesting antiquities both of which lie a little to the west of the direct way through the park. On entering the park, instead of descending into the low-lying haughland by the riverside turn left and climb up the path which leads up a grassy tree-dotted slope to the Motte of Tillydrone, a mound which has its origin as a 'motte' or fortified earthwork and timber castle of the eleventh century.

This was one of four similar mottes on the outskirts of Aberdeen dating from the days of the early Norman penetration of the area, the others (now no longer visible) being at Nigg, Ruthrieston and Gilcomston. They were of the identical type of the primitive timber castles introduced into Britain by William the Conqueror in 1066 and subsequently spread all over the island wherever Norman feudalism took root.

Today of course the Motte of Tillydrone is simply a grass-covered knoll but its very shape proclaims its origin as an artificial earth-work, and its site, affording a fine view, was obviously chosen to command the fords of the river far below it.

A little farther west on the edge of the grassy plateau on which the motte stands is the Wallace Tower or Benholm's Lodging, a fine example of a Scottish Z-plan medieval tower house or castle. It was given the name Wallace Tower from the effigy of a knight (accompanied by a little dog) on an inset panel in one of its two round towers, but in fact it never had any real connection with Sir William Wallace, the Liberator of Scotland.

Z-plan castles had not yet been invented in Wallace's day. They began to make their appearance in the middle of the fifteenth century and take their name from the Z-like shape given by a central block with flanking towers at diagonally opposite angles. Each tower, with its gunloops provided cover to the whole of the main block, which in its turn covered the towers, thus making it impossible to approach such a castle without coming within range of the defenders' fire. This efficient defensive design endeared itself to small lairds in medieval Scotland and 170 of these castles still survive up and down the country.

The Wallace Tower, then, was built in 1616, not on this site but in what is now the centre of 'new' Aberdeen' but was then just outside the built up area, on the Netherkirkgate, leading to St. Nicholas Church. The man who built it was also Laird of Benholm in Kincardine, hence the name Benholm's Lodging. On this central site it remained for 347 years, though suffering partial concealment by neighbouring buildings and some deterioration, until, in 1963, as the result of a development scheme, it was taken down, transported to Tillydrone, and rebuilt practically stone for stone by Aberdeen Corporation in its present position. Thus what had become a familiar landmark to generations of Aberdonians was rescued from oblivion and remains to edify future generations.

We may now retrace our steps and descend into the haughland part of Seaton Park, and pursue the path along the right bank of the River Don which at first follows the loop of the stream opposite Gordon's Mills (the veritable 'crook' of the shepherd's staff). In this open reach the Don picturesquely foams over boulders before it enters the dark, almost sinister, heavily tree-lined gorge of Balgownie.

To the right of the path here stood a handsome eighteenth century mansion, Seaton House, built in 1715 (it is believed to plans by James Gibbs, that great architect son of Aberdeen who was responsible for many famous buildings in England including St. Martins-in-the-Fields in London). Unfortunately it was destroyed by fire in 1963 not long after it had been acquired along with its policies from the Hays of Seaton to form the present park.

The path continues now along the high right bank of the Balgownie gorge with the high plateau of Hillhead of Seaton, now occupied by a series of student halls of residence, immediately to the east and south, and emerges at length on to the final curving sweep of Don Street where it descends to the ancient Brig o' Balgownie.

Here there is a charming group of buildings of varying dates all of which have now been restored. By their old-world air they prepare the visitor for the piquant medieval architecture of the bridge itself. The most important of these is the one we meet first, since we skirt its little garden on the path from Seaton Park just where it joins Don Street. It is called the Chapter House — a complete misnomer, since the very idea of a chapter house at such a fantastic distance from the Cathedral is ludicrous — but the name, fortunately or unfortunately has stuck. In actual fact this pleasant L-plan building with its arched pend surmounted by a coat of arms should be called the Cruickshank Lodging for it was built between 1653 and 1655 by George Cruickshank of Berriehill and his wife Barbara Hervie of Elrick, whose initials G. C. and B. H. along with the date 1655 appear along with their coat of arms over the pend arch.

William Orem, town clerk of Old Aberdeen, in his book on the burgh of his day, tells us that George Cruickshank, who was heritor of the old Manse of Clatt in the Chanonry "carried away some of the stones and other materials to build his house at the Bridge of Don, for accommodating him the time of his fishing".

That this was indeed the function of the house is confirmed from the fact that from the garden a short flight of rough hewn steps leads down the rocky bank to a small jetty on the river, and another of the old houses on this stretch is appropriately enough called "Rocky Bank".

George Cruickshank's name appears frequently in the burgh records of 'new' Aberdeen and in 1644 he was elected Dean of Guild. He and Barbara Hervie had two sons (both born in the Bridge of Don house) and Barbara died there in childbirth in 1689. Their son George Cruickshank, Jr. became a magistrate of Aberdeen, started the first coffee house in the city in 1700, and in 1715 went "out" in the first Jacobite Rebellion and collected "cess" or taxes for the Old Pretender. His brother William appears to have been more prudent. He became Provost of Aberdeen in 1728-29.

THE BRIG O' BALGOWNIE

With a glance at charming Brig House, on the other side of Don Street, and at the remaining old houses on the cobbled approach to the historic bridge let us now look at this famous landmark. If there is one image that has borne the fame of Aberdeen all over the world, and inscribed itself deep in the hearts of all Aberdonians it is the Brig o' Balgownie. Next to the Cathedral of St. Machar it is our greatest monument of the middle ages.

The bridge, 72 feet wide at the water level and 60 feet high to the top of the gracefully pointed Gothic arch, with its long massively buttressed approaches from the south, was completed in 1329.

Robert the Bruce, it used to be said, was the real driving force behind the project, so that Henry Cheyne, Bishop of Aberdeen from 1281 to 1329, was induced to finance the job, from the revenues of his See, during the period of the War of Independence when he had been absent in England.

But it is now thought that work upon the bridge began long before King Robert's day — around 1286 — and that two early Provosts of Aberdeen, Richard Cementarius (Richard the Mason) and Malcolm de Pelgounie or Balgownie were the moving spirits although Cheyne must have given it his blessing. It is thought that Richard the Mason was employed on the building of the Keep of Drum in the 1280's and that the topmost vault in the castle is identical with the Balgownie Arch.

It looks very much as though Richard Cementarius, after he had completed the Tower of Drum quietly moved the centring or scaffolding framework from Deeside to Don at Balgownie and used it to build up the arch of the bridge.

Another intriguing question about the origin of the bridge stems from the famous oracular rhyme — attributed to Thomas the Rhymer (Thomas of Ercildoune):

> Brig o' Balgownie, wicht's thy wa'.
> Wi' a wife's ae son an' a mare's ae foal
> Doon shalt thou fa'.

Now if Thomas really wrote the prophecy the Brig must have been at least partially built in his lifetime, and as he was born in 1220 he must have been long dead by the time of its completion in 1329. The poet Byron was an only son and he rode over the bridge on a pony — presumably a mare's only foal — which had been given him by his mother. The dire prophecy haunted his imagination so much that he recalled it near the end of his life in a letter to a friend.

The upkeep of the bridge caused some anxiety in the first 276 years of its existence but in 1605 there came the modest benefaction of Sir Alexander Hay of Whytburgh whose feu duties of £27 8s 8d (Scots) or £2 5s 6d Sterling went on growing and growing as the value of his Aberdeen properties increased so that there was always enough in the Bridge Fund to ensure the Brig o' Balgownie's safety.

When the new Bridge of Don was built in 1830 the whole cost of £16,000 was met from Sir Alexander Hay's fund. The Brig o' Balgownie was put in a state to last for another 150 years and there was still so much money over that it was proposed to build schools with it.

However a number of citizens objected to this plan, which was then effectively vetoed by the Court of Session. So the fund went on growing. In

May 1972 the balance of monies to the credit of the fund stood at £55,211 and it will doubtless have increased considerably since then.

Across the bridge interest in history may be gratified by a glance at the Cot Town of Balgownie, whose ancient red-tiled cottages in Bridge Terrace have been very finely restored by a private developer. The oldest of them is the one nearest the Brig. Originally known as the Black Nook Alehouse it dates from around 1600.

Sir Alexander Hay's bequest is commemorated by a plaque on a buttress of the Brig. This bears the benefactor's arms and initials. The Latin inscription tells how in the year 1605 "for the love he had for the public good" he bequeathed £27 8s 8d (Scots) to be paid annually from certain lands in Aberdeen "for the purpose of keeping up the building".

BRIG O'
BALGOWNIE
over 600 years
old and still in
daily use

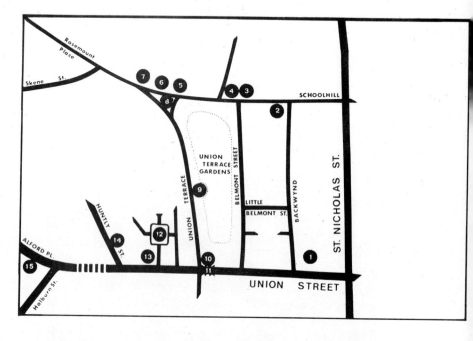

This Map covers Chapter III (pages 49-70)

THE ITEMS OF INTEREST DO NOT NECESSARILY FOLLOW THE EDITORIAL ORDER.

1 St. Nicholas Church
2 James Dun's House
3 Gordons College & Statues
4 Art Gallery, War Memorial &
   Cowdray Hall
5 His Majesty's Theatre
6 South Church (St. Marks)
7 Public Library
8 William Wallace and Prince Consort's statues

9   Burns Statue
10 Edward VII Statue
11 Union Bridge
12 Lord George Gordon
13 Music Hall
14 St. Mary's R.C. Cathedral
15 Christ's College

CHAPTER III
UNION STREET : PIVOT OF MODERN ABERDEEN

To perambulate Union Street from end to end is what the people of Aberdeen and their country cousins from the whole of the north-east of Scotland have done for fully a century and a half, with a special sense of pride and satisfaction, for Union Street is Aberdeen's Royal Mile. It is by no means so historic in a national sense as Edinburgh's famous Old Town thoroughfare, but it is the apotheosis of the Granite City phase in Aberdeen's development. So before we start out on the long walk a word of historical introduction is necessary.

Despite many more spectacular instances of the breed fathered by the twentieth century, Aberdeen is justified in claiming Union Street as one of the earliest and finest fly-overs in the world. Yet it conceals its true nature so effectively that many people walk along Union Street quite unaware that it is a fly-over at all. Only when they descend the Back Wynd Steps, or look down from Union Street over the railings upon the passage far below leading from Correction Wynd to East Green, or note the six storeys of building below street level at the east end of Union Bridge, can they see anything of the tremendous engineering achievement that propelled Aberdeen from the middle ages into the modern world and sent the burgh bankrupt in 1817.

Fully half a mile of Union Street (from Adelphi to Diamond Street) is an artificial creation raised at the lowest from 20 feet to over 50 feet above the natural level of the ground. Aberdeen's New Streets Plan of the last decade of the eighteenth century has often been compared to the building of the New Town of Edinburgh, but in Edinburgh the New Town was laid out on virgin ground on the north side of the Nor' Loch, whilst in Aberdeen a pre-existing town had to be re-made on the spot by tearing down existing buildings, levelling the top of a hill and bridging two valleys. The only valid comparison is with the reconstruction of the centre of Newcastle, which took place about the same time.

It was Charles Abercrombie, engineer of turnpike roads in Aberdeenshire, who first put forward the proposal that Aberdeen should make a new highway through the north side of the Castlegate, bridging the defile known as Putachieside (through which ran the Burn of the Loch), and then the deeper and wider valley of the Den Burn to the west of it, so forcing a way to the "extensive plain to the west of the town".

Long debates, several public meetings, and finally a Parliamentary Bill had to follow before at last the relevant Act of Parliament was passed on April 4, 1800. What were called the Viaduct Approaches were designed by David Hamilton and Charles Abercrombie and begun in 1800. They consisted of a series of arches from Adelphi to Union Bridge and from Union Bridge to Diamond Street. The spanning of the deep and wide chasm of the Den Burn was recognised from the first to be the major link in the whole operation and was approached with due deliberation. The

Shirras Laing

In 1829 James Laing set up business as an ironmonger at No. 100 Union Street, later moving to No 98 and to No. 121. In 1849, as James Laing and Co., the firm expanded the sphere of its work to include bell-hanging and working in iron and a workshop was established first at Flourmill Lane and then at No. 10 Back Wynd.

From an oil contract dated 1880, there is evidence that William Shirres (late Shirras), in 1841, set up business at No. 5 Hanover Street as a tinsmith, moving in 1850 to No. 18 Upperkirkgate. In 1865 Shirres moved to Nos. 42-44 Schoolhill, still retaining his former premises. His son (George Findlay) joined the firm in 1880 under the title of William Shirras and Son.

The two firms, James Laing and Co. and William Shirras and Son, amalgamated circa 1885 to form Shirras Laing and Co., operating from both Schoolhill and Upperkirkgate as tinsmiths and electrical engineers. The present building was designed and built for the new company around 1890 by John Rust, the first City Architect and the Town's Superintendent for Works, and the company became a limited company in 1898. The firm employed a large staff of tinsmiths and made most of the street lanterns for Aberdeen as well as a range of railway and domestic oil lamps. It is believed to have been the first electrical contractor in the city, wiring such buildings as the Town House and Marischal College, but the Directors declared in 1902 that their Electric Light Department was "still unremunerative". The first Royal Warrant was granted to the Company in 1889 by Queen Victoria.

SCHOOLHILL   ABERDEEN   Telephone 25242

first idea was for a bridge of three arches, and unexecuted plans for this by Sir John Rennie, David Hamilton of Glasgow and James Young of London survive. Then Thomas Telford was consulted and proposed a bridge of 150 ft. in a single span in a drawing submitted on February 3, 1802. Telford's plan was not adopted in its entirety. The real architect of the bridge was Thomas Fletcher, whose finished design resulted in a bridge of granite ashlar of 132 ft. span and two built-up arches each of 50 feet. Work began in 1802 and was completed in 1805.

Although the filling up of Union Street with houses was a slow process, only completed over half a century, its essential character was laid down in the first two decades of the nineteenth century. The houses at the eastern end of the street were given great uniformity, generally as four-storey and attic blocks in fine granite ashlar. Today Union Street is Aberdeen's Conservation Area No. 2 (No. 1 as already mentioned being Old Aberdeen). It contains over 50 buildings or groups of buildings — excluding the public landmarks, the Music Hall and the screen of St. Nicholas Kirk — which are scheduled in the Secretary of State's list of structures of architectural interest. To the informed eye Union Street is a history book of the golden age of granite-city building, and buildings from the earliest and finest period of the nineteenth century, before or around 1820 are to be found from end to end. One may move up and down Union Street and savour the work of virtually all the great Aberdeen architects — Archibald Simpson, John and William Smith, James Matthews, A. Marshall Mackenzie, right down to A. G. R. Mackenzie and Jenkins and Marr in our own day. There is just one qualification to this. In most cases (but not in every case) one has to try to ignore what the Secretary of State's list calls "the modern ground floor shop fronts". They are later insertions, geared to the tastes of a public more interested in spotting a bargain than in savouring period architecture.

We are now ready to begin our walk in Union Street and there is no better place to start than the Town House corner of Union Street and Broad Street. This is where, in 1800, the city-builders sliced through the top of the ancient St. Katherine's Hill and the now-vanished Narrow Wynd, to join up Union Street to the west end of Castle Street.

Take your stand at the Town House corner and look across the street. Immediately facing you is the massive Union Street facade of Union Buildings, Nos. 5-21 Union Street. This is the Union Street frontage of the same block which (at Nos. 1 and 2 Castle Street) contains the Royal Athenaeum building, but here it presents a quite different aspect. Built to designs by Archibald Simpson between 1819-22 it is of four storeys and an attic with a range of eleven windows on each floor facing Union Street. The centre five windows are 'advanced', that is projected forward slightly, and surmounted by a classical swagged wallhead panel. Originally all the windows on the ground floor were arched, and you can still see a line of six of them at the east end of the frontage.

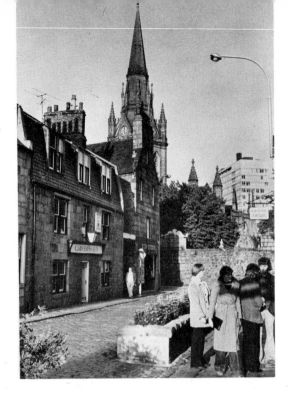

Left: LITTLE BELMONT STREET with St.
Nicholas Church in the background
Below: ST. NICHOLAS CHURCHYARD

It was of the severe elegance of this style of building that "Smith's Guide to Aberdeen" was thinking when it said of Union Street in 1836 — "the simplicity and chasteness of its architecture will make no inconsiderable figure when compared with the best streets of any city in the Kingdom", adding "you cannot fail to be struck with the air of plainness and with the want of tawdry display which is so offensive in the shops of most other towns".

Another Archibald Simpson range of buildings of an even earlier date is to be seen on the north (or right-hand side) of the street at Nos. 46-50. This building, collectively called Union Chambers, was built in 1811 as a four-storey and attic block with a five-storey four-window centre, with the wallhead raised over each pair and chaimneys above the windows being architraved.

As it begins its career on hidden arches west of Adelphi, the cul-de-sac street entered by a pend arch on the south side just before No. 55, Union Street slopes gently down to the Market Street - St. Nicholas Street intersection. Here the two bank buildings facing each other on the north side are each of special interest. They demonstrate how architectural styles have changed, but can still be reconciled to the plain Regency style of the original pattern.

Nos. 60-62, the Clydesdale Bank, is a work of James Matthews in the Renaissance style of which he was particularly fond, with decoration of the giant Corinthian pilaster order at the two lower floors and red granite details at the centre door and the first floor of the end bays. This building was built in 1862. Across the way on the other side of St. Nicholas Street, Nos. 78-80 the Royal Bank, dates only from 1936, but at that time granite was still being extensively used for public buildings and here the architects, Jenkins and Marr, have achieved a spectacular effect with the giant order of unfluted Corinthian columns rising through ground, first and second floors.

In the next stretch of Union Street, moving west, a very pleasing break in the normal sequence of commercial facades is provided by a great classical screen separating Union Street from St. Nicholas Kirkyard. This dates from 1830 and was designed by John Smith, City Architect of Aberdeen, as a revision of a more elaborate scheme by Decimus Burton. It is an Ionic colonnade in light grey granite, 147 feet long, with centre archway. The cast iron work of the railings between the pillars and in the gateway is considered very fine.

In summer, trees cast the green flourish of their branches over the pediment and invite the passer-by to enter the Kirkyard itself, where he will find plentiful seats appropriate for a picnic lunch or a quiet pause for reflection. At the height of the summer lunchtime entertainments are sometimes organised here. Many of the monuments in the churchyard repay close study. As one enters the arched gateway one cannot help noticing a massive classical monument with four Grecian Doric columns enclosing a sculptured urn. They commemorate Professor Hamilton of

Marischal College, an expert on the National Debt. The existing enclosing walls and gates of St. Nicholas Kirk in the four streets which surround it — Union Street, Back Wynd (along the western boundary), Schoolhill (along the northern boundary) and Correction Wynd (along the eastern boundary) are all protected monuments in themselves — all being listed in the Secretary of State for Scotland's schedules of "buildings of historic importance".

Back Wynd, the street immediately west of the churchyard, connecting Union Street with Schoolhill on the north, is very old. Formerly known as Westerkirkgate, it was laid out by the magistrates in 1594.

In the following century the massive rubble-built wall along the greater part of the east side of the Back Wynd, separating it from the Kirkyard, was built and against it were placed a whole succession of baroque monuments and tombs. Some of these monuments, which are interesting period works of art have already suffered from vandalism, although the beautiful Rickart memorial is one that has been specially treated and carefully preserved. Dated 1696 its sculptured angels, decorative scroll-work and carvings of skeletons, and skulls and crossbones remain to remind us of the elaborite funerary fancies of our ancestors.

ST. NICHOLAS CHURCH

St. Nicholas Church is the ancient burgh church of Aberdeen. Aberdeen is not unique in having chosen St. Nicholas, the friend of sailors, as its patron saint. He is the patron saint also of Newcastle, Berwick, Amsterdam, Hamburg, and Keil, all North Sea trading communities. But it is unusual that the burgh church of Aberdeen stood in the middle ages apart and outside the burgh boundaries, on the west side of the declivity formed by the Burn of the Loch, while, the rest of the town clustered behind its walls and gates or 'Ports' on the east side. An attempt has been made to explain this by suggesting that early in the twelfth century the earliest location of the burgh was on the axis formed by the Kirk of St. Nicholas and the Green, running down to the point where the Den Burn entered the harbour, and that this site was changed in favour of the Castlegate and the east side of St. Katherine's Hill after the Vikings under King Eynstein of Norway had burned and wasted the little town in 1153.

At all events it is clear that Aberdeen's Kirk of St. Nicholas existed in 1151 when it is mentioned in a Bull of Pope Adrian IV — Nicholas Brakespear, the only British occupant of the Chair of St. Peter — addressed to Edward, Bishop of Aberdeen. The transepts of this original edifice remain — with some alterations it is true — but they show a series of plain round-headed, deep-splayed windows, now blocked up, and two low archways leading formerly into the main aisles, which in their extreme severity are suggestive of a date considerably earlier than the first year of Bishop Edward — 1150. If one assumes that the Kirk was burned as well as the town in 1153, this affords a tempting explanation of certain

Opposite: HIS MAJESTY'S THEATRE, ST. MARK'S CHURCH (formerly South Chu

Transitional features which are found in close juxtaposition to the Norman work — the four arches under the central tower, and small windows on the east wall of the north transept, as well as two slender engaged shafts, with characteristic capitals, which fortunately have been retained in the side of the sixteenth century window in the gable of that transept.

The main path running through St. Nicholas Kirkyard from Union Street leads straight to the great door under the steeple giving entry to the transepts and the crossing, by far the oldest part of the surviving church, which has suffered from many vicissitudes down its long history. In the middle ages it was the largest burgh church in Scotland, consisting of nave and aisles, transepts, an aisled chancel of three bays with semi-circular apse and a central tower, the whole length being 256 feet. At the Reformation this historic building was divided into two separate places of worship, the East Church, occupying the chancel and the West Church occupying the nave. Both have since been rebuilt as has the central tower.

As it stands today, however, there are still some treasured ancient features. The transepts are mainly late twelfth century Transitional, with round crossing arches, piers with foliage, caps and square abaci. The South Transept, known as Drum's Aisle, which one enters from the great main door, contains a stone effigy of Sir Alexander Irvine of Drum, who died in 1457, and also a monumental brass. This transept was refaced externally by Archibald Simpson in 1835-7 and there were further repairs after the great fire which destroyed the central tower in 1874. These were carried out between 1875 and 1877 by William Smith. It was Smith who also designed the present Gothic central tower with spire. The belfry of this tower houses a carillon of 48 bells which regularly peal out psalm tunes that can be heard above the clamour of the city's traffic.

The North Transept, known as Collison's Aisle, was remodelled in the seventeenth century, though the ancient features mentioned above were retained alongside the great window in the north gable with its fine basket tracery or lead apron, which is dated 1518.

There also survives the lovely medieval crypt under the East Church, completed shortly before 1438 by Aberdeen's Master of Kirk Work, Sir Andro Wricht. It is on a three-bay plan with rib and groin vault under the eastmost bay and apse of the East Church. Known in the earlier records as Our Lady of Pity's Vault, its exterior was refaced by Archibald Simpson in 1835-7 and its collection of fifteenth and sixteenth century woodwork restored by Dr. William Kelly in 1898. As restored it is now known as St. Mary's Chapel and is entered by an external door from Correction Wynd, on the low-level east side of the kirk.

The East Church itself which had been designed by Archibald Simpson and built in 1835-7 was gutted in the fire of 1874 and rebuilt (on the foundations of the medieval choir) by William Smith in 1875-7. It is in the Gothic style, of granite ashlar, with freestone tracery.

Mention has been made already (in dealing with Seaton Park) of the most famous architect son of Aberdeen, James Gibbs, designer of St. Martins-in-the-Fields and other notable works in England. The one surviving work of Gibbs in Aberdeen itself is the present West Church of St. Nicholas, entered from a gateway in Back Wynd. He designed the church in 1741 but it was not actually built until 1751-5 under the supervision of James Wyllie of Edinburgh. Among the last buildings in Aberdeen to be built of sandstone, it is in a Renaissance style of five bays with aisles, having arched openings with Gibbs' surrounds at door and central window. The interior is barrel-vaulted with aisles groin-vaulted and arcades with R-doric pilasters. The church retains the original pulpit and sounding board.

In the church are preserved four tapestries with Biblical themes, the work of Mary Jamesone, daughter of George Jamesone, the 'Father' of Scottish portrait painting, and grand-daughter of the architect of Provost Ross's House. Among the interesting memorials in the church is the Allardyce Monument by J. Benson (1791).

BELMONT STREET AND LITTLE BELMONT STREET

The buildings in Back Wynd are not of any special note save for the one at the Back Wynd - Union Street corner now occupied by shops and the Cinema House. This, Nos. 114-122 Union Street and No. 1 Back Wynd, was designed by John Smith in 1836-7 as Advocates Hall and was occupied by the Aberdeen Society of Advocates from then until 1872, when they moved to their new hall in Concert Court, already described. It is an imposing three-storey curved corner block with Ionic columns of the anta-order and pediment to Back Wynd. As Smith had recently designed the St. Nicholas Kirkyard screen he very properly continued the Ionic theme in this neighbouring structure.

Half way along its length Back Wynd is linked to Belmont Street by a short street called Little Belmont Street which, because of its site, gives interesting perspective views of St. Nicholas Kirk and steeple.

On the north side of the street is a charming little building in the classical style, one of the gems of early granite construction. It too was built by John Smith. It is on a single storey E-plan with a tetrastyle unfluted G-doric colonnade between the wings, surmounted by a massive pediment. At first known as the Old Town School it later became an annexe to the Aberdeen Academy and is now used by the Schools' Music Department. It dates from 1841.

Little Belmont Street and Belmont Street, to which it gives access from Back Wynd, were originally formed in 1784, two decades before Union Street itself, and so contain several late eighteenth century buildings, notably Nos. 25, 37 and 37a and 47 Belmont Street. At the back of No. 25 Belmont Street in the courtyard facing down into the Denburn Valley are to be seen two interesting heraldic pieces. One is a panel showing the coat of arms and crest of Thomas Menzies of Pitfodels who was Provost of Aberdeen in 1525, and the other is a coat of arms of the Irvine of Drum family. The Menzies panel came from the Castlegate to its present site in 1806.

There are churches on both sides of Belmont Street. On the east side at the corner of Little Belmont Street is the former South Parish Church of St. Nicholas built to John Smith's design in 1830-31 in neo-perpendicular granite ashlar, with wood tracery on a T-plan with front tower. It has now been converted into a suite of halls for the Church of Scotland and re-named Kirk House.

On the other side of the street is Belmont Congregational Church. This was built to plans by William Leslie in 1865 in the Italian Romanesque style with flanking towerlets and entrance at an east apse, with eaves gallery flanked by towerlets on the west overlooking the Denburn Valley.

On the west side of Belmont Street at its northern end, at its junction with Schoolhill, is the massive ecclesiastical complex originally known as the Triple Kirks, originally built to designs by Archibald Simpson in 1844 to house three Disruption churches which emerged from the St. Nicholas congregations, and now occupied by East and Belmont Church (entered from 67 Schoolhill) and the former Albion and St. Paul's Congregational Church (entering from 71 Schoolhill).

The Triple Kirks are in the Early Pointed Gothic style, rubble-built with brick dressings and with a great brick spire, modelled on that of Marburg Cathedral, which dominates the Denburn Valley.

Plans have been approved for the reconstruction of the Triple Kirks for commercial use, but the magnificent brick spire will be retained.

Facing the Triple Kirks on the east side of old Belmont Street and extending eastwards along Schoolhill is the old Aberdeen Academy building designed by J. Ogg Allan as the Central School, for Aberdeen School Board, in 1901. It is a handsome three-storey Renaissance-style block with leaded corner dome and R-doric columns at windows. There are Venetians with in-and-out voussoirs at top floor, with arched tops raised in the roof. The Aberdeen Academy itself, one of Aberdeen's most important secondary comprehensive schools moved to Hazlehead on the western outskirts of the city in 1970 and was re-named Hazlehead Academy on becoming a 'neighbourhood comprehensive' whilst the original building is now a general annexe used by the education department.

UNION TERRACE AND ITS GARDENS

Constantly I have had to refer to the Denburn Valley in the previous paragraphs, for Belmont Street perches on the high bank which fronts it on the east. We will now return to the Union Street end of Belmont Street and see how Union Street itself crosses this great natural feature, and the civic use that has been made of it.

Between Belmont Street and Union Bridge are two buildings which call for mention. Nos. 136-144 Union Street was originally built by Archibald Simpson in 1826-27 as the Aberdeen Hotel, a simple comely

Opposite: WILLIAM WALLACE STATUE in bro...

granite ashlar block showing a three-storey, six-window frontage to Union Street but seven storeys to the Denburn Valley, where it fronts Denburn Road. It is now occupied by shops and the Victoria Restaurant. Here is the typical Union Street plainness with dignity. Across the street, on the south side, but also partly fronting the Denburn Valley, there is a very striking contrast for here at Nos. 151-155 Union Street is Old Trinity Hall designed in an elaborate Tudor Gothic style by John and William Smith in 1846.

Buildings like this have given John Smith his nickname 'Tudor Johnnie', and it is said to have impressed the Prince Consort so much that he gave John Smith's son and partner William the commission to design Balmoral Castle. This Trinity Hall, built to house the headquarters of the Seven Incorporated Trades of Aberdeen has a two storey frontage on Union Street but descends six stories to Denburn Road and the Green, and built into the Denburn Road portion is a fragment of the still older Trinity Hall, which was the original home of the Trades, dated 1633.

It is rather sad to have to record that the Incorporated Trades, finding that the absence of car parking facilities attached to the building was a handicap in the twentieth century, felt impelled to give up this historic home and build themselves a new Trinity Hall in Holburn Street.

We now come to Union Bridge itself which, as we saw earlier, was designed by Thomas Fletcher and completed in its original form in 1805. But there have been two subsequent major operations on the bridge which have quite transformed its simple granite outlines. In the years from 1905 to 1908 the bridge was widened to plans by William Dyack with Benjamin Baker as consultant. The familiar steel spans of today were introduced then, while new parapets were designed by Dr. William Kelly, whose leopard finials (still to be seen on the north parapet only) were christened Kelly's Cats. Finally the bridge was further widened and shops added to the south side in 1964.

Some people regret that the shops, however convenient, closed a view down the valley to the south, with the rising ground on the far side of the Dee in the distance, but the view to the north was always the finer and it remains, giving a delightful prospect over Union Terrace Gardens, a much-frequented public park laid out in grassy slopes and flower beds alongside the railway line to the north — in much the same way as Princes Street Gardens utilise the former bed of the Nor' Loch in Edinburgh.

Until the coming of the railway between 1863 and 1867 this open space was centred by the Den Burn running open to the view and was known as Corbie Heugh, the Crow's Copse, because of the rooks that frequented the wooded banks of the valley. The Den Burn still runs, but unseen in an underground culvert, yet the rooks have remained. A mighty colony of them may still be seen rearing their young in the trees of Union Terrace Gardens close to the busy traffic junction of Union Street.

Let us pause for a moment on Union Bridge to enjoy a view of which Aberdonians seldom tire. On the far side of the long green hollow of Union

Terrace, with its grassy lawns and trees and flowerbeds, the prospect is closed by a fine range of buildings along the line of Schoolhill Viaduct. These are the Central Public Library, above which the new skyscraper of the Upper Denburn high flats now soars, St. Mark's Church and His Majesty's Theatre—a trio nicknamed of old 'Education, Salvation and Damnation'.

St. Mark's has a massive, and the theatre a miniature dome, and this theme of domes is repeated farther along Schoolhill and the area just behind it by the dome of Archibald Simpson's handsome neo-classical Old Infirmary building (now in use as an outpatient department) and by the dome of the Cowdray Hall, the War Memorial and the Art Gallery, which form a single continuous block.

This whole complex of buildings, which the eye can take in at a single sweep is a striking answer to those who complain of the severity of the granite as a building material.

Now let us move on to the west end of the bridge, where Alfred Drury's massive granite statue of King Edward VII, flanked by bronze groups representing the triumphs of peace, forms a stately terminal feature at the corner of Union Terrace. It dates from 1914.

On the opposite side of Union Terrace at its junction with Union Street is another of those fine corner blocks with semi-circular pillared portico which are so characteristic of nineteenth century Aberdeen. This one, the Northern Assurance, latterly the Commercial Union building, was designed by A. Marshall Mackenzie in 1885. Rather incongruously it has been nicknamed "the Monkey House", doubtless because of its usefulness as a sheltered rendezvous-point for dating couples.

Moving along Union Terrace we find some interesting contrasts in architectural styles. No. 16, with its large fanlight, dates from the eighteenth century and is probably the oldest house in the street. But beyond it we come to four massive blocks displaying elaborate Renaissance style frontages and extending from No. 19 to No. 25. All were built between 1896 and 1902.

The Aberdeen Savings Bank (No. 19) is an essay in the Italian Renaissance style by Dr. William Kelly (1896). No. 22 was originally designed by A. Marshall Mackenzie for the Aberdeen School Board. The building has a five-bay, three storey and basement front with R-doric and buttress features on the first floor, while the ground floor is arched and rusticated.

No. 20, between it and the Savings Bank, was also designed by Marshall Mackenzie and built in 1897 for the Aberdeen City Parish Council, whose insignia is still there for all to see on the glass front door. This building is also three storeys with R-doric columns at the top floor, the two lower floors being banded with bands running through an imposing two-storey R-doric entrance porch. No. 25 Union Terrace, built in 1902 was designed by A. G. Sydney and Wilson and consists of a four-storey and attic five-bay elevation, with the centre at first and second floors recessed between R-doric pilasters. There is a Gibbs surround to the first floor windows and the ground floor is rusticated).

Promenaders however, usually choose the open side of Union Terrace — and here one of the most remarkable features is the very long granite balustrade with its plump and rounded supporting pillars, identical with the original parapet of Union Bridge. Here too is a famous statue of Robert Burns, Scotland's national bard, holding in his hand the daisy which he apostrophised as "wee, crimson-tipped floo'er". This handsome bronze figure on its lofty pedestal of granite was the work of Henry Bainsmith and dates from 1892. The daisy itself has been so often removed by vandals that its replacement became a labour of supererogation. The long series of arches supporting the pavement and parapet of Union Terrace from the level of the Gardens below was completed in 1892 when the street was widened by 21 feet.

Of rather more recent date is the cluster of open-air giant draughts boards on the lower terrace, always a popular entertainment in the summer months, while pipe bands and concert parties draw admiring crowds to the seating around the bandstand in the gardens below. The arms of the city laid out in floral beds on the grassy slope at the north end delight the eye with a splash of heraldic colour.

Aberdeen's valhalla of the famous in this corner of the town is completed by Count Carlo Marochetti's seated bronze figure of Albert the Prince Consort, which was originally unveiled by Queen Victoria in 1863, and the enormous bronze statue of Sir William Wallace, Scotland's Liberator, a work by W. Grant Stevenson dating from 1888. There Wallace stands, upon a massive red granite plinth, with his great sword in his right hand, his left arm extended in a gesture pointing across Schoolhill to His Majesty's Theatre — an architectural tour de force undreamed of when he first took up his stand.

At this northern end of Union Terrace the present configuration of the townscape demanded massive engineering works — the construction of Rosemount Viaduct and Denburn Viaduct, both of which were built in 1886 under the 1883 Aberdeen Extension and Improvements Act. Designed by William Boulton, the Rosemount Viaduct is a great segmented skew arch of bullfaced granite over the Upper Denburn valley, while Denburn Viaduct has three similar arches on quoined bullfaced piers spanning the Lower Denburn valley and linking Rosemount Viaduct to Schoolhill.

Once this job had been done the way was open for the building of the Public Library and St. Mark's Church, both completed in 1892, the latter with its massive Corinthian portico and dome being the work of A. Marshall Mackenzie.

Aberdeen is justly proud of His Majesty's Theatre, built in 1906 to designs by Frank Matcham. The frontage is of white Kemnay granite and the rest of the building of pink Tilliefourie granite. It has an excellent claim to being the finest theatre in Scotland. The frieze above the stage was by W. H. Buchan, while in niches above the boxes are life-size figures of Tragedy and Comedy. It was bought by Aberdeen Town Council in January, 1974 to ensure its future as a theatre.

Crossing the Denburn Viaduct and with the Triple Kirks and the old Aberdeen Academy buildings (already described) on our right, we face the Cowdray Hall, the War Memorial and the Art Gallery. This complex of buildings has arisen through successive extensions of the original Art Gallery in Schoolhill, a pink granite building in the Italian Renaissance style dating from 1885. The rugged granite lion on its pedestal within the War Memorial frontage was the work of an Aberdeen sculptor, William Macmillan R.A., who designed the World War I Victory Medal, while the Cowdray Hall adjoining was opened in 1925 and was the gift of the first Viscountess Cowdray. In the basement beneath the War Memorial Shrine is an excellent regional museum.

Aberdeen Art Gallery, entered from Schoolhill, has one of the finest art collections in Britain. Generous endowment has enabled it to amass a catholic and up-to-date permanent holding, while up to five visiting exhibitions are on view simultaneously at the gallery and concerts, recitals, lectures and cultural events of many kinds are frequently held. Visitors should make a point of obtaining the monthly programmes of the Gallery which list these attractions.

Very well represented in the permanent collection are works of the Scottish School from George Jamesone (1588-1644), the Father of Scottish Portrait Painting, who himself lived and worked in Schoolhill, and left to Aberdeen its first public park, the Four-neukit Garden, the only surviving fragment of which is the historic Well of Spa in nearby Spa Street, to Sir William MacTaggart and many others of our own day. Among the Aberdeen artists James Giles has already been mentioned. He was followed by William Dyce of Pre-Raphaelite fame and John ('Spanish') Philip, and it was in thinking of this celebrated nineteenth century trio that James Cassie, another prominent Aberdeen artist gave voice to the familiar Aberdeen boast: "There's Jamesone, Dyce and Philip — tak' awa' Aberdeen an' twal' mile roon an' far are ye?" (Take away Aberdeen and twelve miles round and where are you?).

The French Impressionists and Post-Impressionists and the modern English School are well represented with notable works by Manet, Sisley, Augustus John, W. R. Sickert, Degas, Jack Yeats, Wyndham Lewis and Ben Nicholson, while the sculpture includes several works by Epstein and Henry Moore. Renoir's 'La Roche Guyan' is now on permanent loan from H.M. Government to the Art Gallery.

The street Schoolhill takes its name from the ancient Grammar School of the burgh, founded in the fifteenth century, which formerly stood in this very corner, but moved west to Carden Place in 1863. But the name of the street is still appropriate for the arched gateway to the east of the Art Gallery leads to Gordon's College, the second most ancient school in the city.

It is approached by a long avenue flanked by lawns and the buildings of Robert Gordon's Institute of Technology. The central block, the original building affectionately known as 'The Auld House', was designed by William Adam, father of the better-known Adam Brothers, and completed in 1739. It was founded by Robert Gordon, an Aberdeen merchant trading with the Baltic, as a 'hospital' or boarding school for the sons of poorer burgesses in Aberdeen. It is now a day school (with a small boarding house for the sons of parents living abroad). As a member of the Headmasters' Conference, it is also a 'public school' in the English not the Scottish sense.

Standing in the small railed-off lawn with shrubs and trees in front of the great arch that leads to the College from Schoolhill is a statue of another Gordon, quite unconnected with the Founder. This is General Gordon of Khartoum, the hero and martyr of the British campaign against the Dervishes in Sudan. The bronze figure by T. Stuart Burnett dates from 1888.

Before we leave Schoolhill do take a look at No. 61 on the other side of the street, next door to the Old Aberdeen Academy. This charming Georgian house, recently restored, is Aberdeen's Children's Museum. It is built of hand-dressed granite ashlar, probably from Rubislaw Quarries, with alternate window jambs of a darker stone, which adds interest to the design, and the charm of the fenestration is enhanced by the well-proportioned doorway with its finely moulded architrave. It was built in 1769, when James Dun, Rector of the Grammar School, was granted permission to build a house convenient for himself just opposite to the school, which at that time stood on the other side of the street. The Children's Museum called James Dun's House, is an annexe of the Art Gallery.

WESTERN UNION STREET

We must now return to the Union Street - Union Terrace junction and continue our way westward. This part of the "new Aberdeen" of the early nineteenth century is not quite so splendid as the civic fathers originally intended. They had envisaged that the then open plain beyond Union Bridge would be laid out in the shape of a great parallelogram, bounded by Union Street on the south and by a road on the line of Skene Street on the north, extending from Union Terrace on the east to Alford Place on the west and enclosing spacious streets and squares between.

Only part of this scheme actually eventuated, but in Golden Square we can see what was intended, in sample, so to speak. Most of the simple, dignified granite ashlar houses in Golden Square, best approached by South Silver Street, the second opening on the right as we proceed up Union Street, were built before 1821. Unfortunately, the once lovely lawn in the centre of the Square has given way to a convenient car park, centred by the statue of George, fifth and last Duke of Gordon, carved in granite by Thomas Campbell in 1842 and removed from the Castlegate in 1952 after standing there 110 years. As more city centre car parking facilities

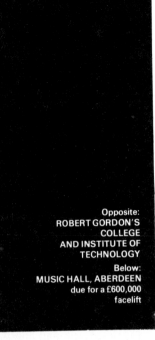

Opposite:
ROBERT GORDON'S
COLLEGE
AND INSTITUTE OF
TECHNOLOGY

Below:
MUSIC HALL, ABERDEEN
due for a £600,000
facelift

become available the centre of Golden Square may be freed of its present congestion and restored to something of its old-time dignity.

Occupying the south-west section of Golden Square, all the west side of South Silver Street and with a show frontage on Union Street itself is the Music Hall, a building with a long and important history in the social annals of Aberdeen. The Union Street facade of the Music Hall, with its six Ionic columns 30 ft. high on a frontage 90 ft. in width dates from 1820 and like much of the interior is the work of Archibald Simpson, who created it as the answer to a long-felt want in the city for public rooms in which genteel 'assemblies' could be held by the aristocracy of the North-east. Hence its original name — the Assembly Rooms.

In the early years of the nineteenth century two attempts by city folk themselves to build new public rooms which would be worthy of the city had to fail before 'the County' stepped in and triumphantly did the job. Their scheme was launched at the race meetings held at the Links in 1818. By the end of that year over £7000 had been raised and a committee of subscribers, all county folk, led by the Duke of Gordon (whose statue we have just noted in Golden Square), was formed with full powers to carry the project through. They advertised for plans offering 50 guineas for the best design. Simpson's plan was chosen. The foundation stone was laid with great ceremony on April 26, 1820 after a procession of 1500 masonic brethren, preceded by a detachment of soldiers and accompanied by the town council and other public bodies had marched from Castle Street to the site. Archibald Simpson marched in the procession carrying the plans in his hand. The foundation stone at the corner of Union Street and South Silver Street bears a plaque with the inscription:

ABERDEEN PUBLIC ROOMS
BUILT BY SUBSCRIPTION FOUNDED WITH MASONIC HONOURS
BY—
JAMES EARL FIFE, DEPUTE GRAND MASTER FOR SCOTLAND,
APRIL 26, 1820, FIRST YEAR OF THE REIGN OF
GEORGE THE FOURTH

Simpson's own description of the interior, couched in the stately language of the period is worth quoting:

"The principal entrance under the portico conducts into an outer vestibule, having a flight of six steps leading to the Grand Salon, which is 46 ft. in length and is divided into three compartments by fluted Ionic columns with ornamental capitals and corresponding pilasters. The centre part is 32 ft. high and the ceiling is a dome finished with coppering. In the centre of the building and opening into the salon through a screen of columns is a spacious gallery or promenade 70 ft. in length, furnished with pilasters and an arched and panelled ceiling.

"It communicates on one side with the Ballroom, which is 70 ft. long, 25 ft. broad and 35 ft. high, with segmentally arched ceiling, and on the other side with the supper or refreshment room (now called the Square Room) which is a square of 34 ft. with a domed ceiling.

"Communicating with this room is the card salon (the Round Room) which is a rotunda. It is decorated with eight fluted Corinthian columns and corresponding pilasters, over which the entablature forms a circle of 34 ft. diameter, from which springs the ceiling in the form of a flat dome with eight compartments intended to be filled with paintings. Within the columns are four spacious recesses for sofas, with niches in the wall."

This elegant suite of rooms, completed in the early part of 1822, served for 36 years the function for which it had been built, but times and fashions changed. The aristocracy who had once flocked to its gilded magnificence found themselves in the railway age drawn to the capital in Edinburgh, and in 1858 the building was sold to the Music Hall Company who sought to give it a new lease of life by adding on to the original suite a banqueting hall to seat from 2000 to 3000 persons. The architect of this new Great Hall was James Matthews, later Lord Provost Matthews, who had been Archibald Simpson's apprentice.

The new hall was opened in style on the evening of September 14, 1859, when the Prince Consort delivered an address as President of the British Association, which met in Aberdeen that year. Since then many famous conferences and many famous political meetings have been held in the Music Hall and as a concert hall it is considered to be among the finest in Britain. Today the Scottish National Orchestra gives a monthly series of concerts here each winter, and the International Festival of Youth Orchestras takes it over for two weeks each August, when over 1000 young musicians come from all over the world.

Opening off the south side of Union Street, opposite the Music Hall are Crown Street (where the older portion of the General Post Office displays a grandiose castellated style) and Dee Street.

A little way along the latter, at the corner of Langstane Place, is the Lang Stane, a granite monolith for which a niche has been provided in the wall of a store. It is probably a survivor of a Bronze Age stone circle. Some distance west on the same line of street, but now called Hardgate, is the Crab Stane, a squarish boulder, also preserved in a special niche. Originally the boundary stone of a croft belonging to John Crab, a Flemish immigrant who became a hero of the War of Independence by inventing a siege weapon called 'the Soo' employed at Berwick. This historic stone also marks the site of two notable battles — the Battle of the Crab Stane, on 20th November 1571, between protagonists and antagonists of Mary Queen of Scots, and the Battle of the Justice Mills, on 'Black Friday', 13th September 1644 — the prelude to the deplorable Sack of Aberdeen by the 'wild Irishes' and Highlanders of the Marquess of Montrose.

The streets on both sides of this western half of Union Street were laid out on land belonging to the various craft guilds of the Seven Incorporated Trades of Aberdeen: Crown Street by the Hammermen, and Bon-Accord Square, Terrace and Crescent farther west by Archibald Simpson for the Tailor Craft. This whole complex of fine residential streets — now largely given over to offices — has been very properly designated a conservation area. Bon-Accord Crescent in particular, with its great sweep of continuous and uniform two storey, basement and attic houses in light grey granite ashlar, would not disgrace the crescents of Bath or Edinburgh New Town.

Bon-Accord Terrace and Crescent stand high, overlooking the great hollow once occupied by the vale of the Howe Burn, and this open space, has been converted into pleasant landscaped parkland, having previously been market gardens. It is interesting to note that Archibald Simpson, the great planner of this whole quarter of the town lived for some time at No. 13-15 Bon-Accord Square and died in a nearby house in East Craibstone Street (the short street linking Bon-Accord Square with Bon-Accord Street) in 1847. A feature of Bon-Accord Street itself is the impressive frontage of Telephone House, the first of Aberdeen's modern buildings in the 'granite city' tradition. It was designed by the London architect Leonard Stokes in 1908.

In the centre of Bon-Accord Square is the 'Muckle Stane of Bon-Accord', a simple granite monolith commemorating Archibald Simpson with the inscription: 'Archibald Simpson, Architect 1790-1847. A Pioneer of Civic Design in this his native city'. It was placed there in 1975 by Aberdeen Civic Society, as a contribution to European Architectural Heritage Year.

The Music Hall is flanked on the west by the modern YMCA building with shops on the ground floor. The entrance is in Huntly Street, the next opening to the north, dominated by the soaring spire and steeple of St. Mary's, the Cathedral of the Roman Catholic diocese of Aberdeen. The building was designed by Alexander Ellis and built in 1859-60 while the spire was designed by his partner R. G. Wilson and added in 1877. Ellis, whose work both in domestic and ecclesiastical architecture was a striking feature of Victorian Aberdeen, gave the cathedral a stately nave with aisles and clerestorey, and dormers in the aisle roofs, while the adjoining clergy house is of two storeys and attic of pinned rubble with V-plan dormers. The statue of St. Mary in its niche facing towards Union Street was by the brilliant young Aberdeen sculptor Alexander Brodie.

In its original form the interior of the cathedral was filled with elaborate decoration and emblems of piety and given a rood beam. This was quite in accord with Victorian ideas of lush ecclesiastical furniture, but two decades ago all this was swept away leaving an effect of austere simplicity. The modern note was emphasised by the long succession of wall mosaic panels depicting the Stations of the Cross, the work of a famous French artist, Gabriele Loire of Chartres, dedicated in September 1969. Opposite the cathedral are the oldest houses in Huntly Street, Nos. 23, 25 and 27, built between 1818 and 1821.

On the south side of Union Street on the site at the west corner of Bon-Accord Street is the Langstane Church, built in 1868-69 to plans by James Matthews. This splendid freestone structure in the Gothic style has a spire 175 ft. high and stands a little back from Union Street so that the paved courtyard can be used for art exhibitions and at Christmas time for a lighted Christmas tree.

At the same time as the Langstane Church was being built another essay in ecclesiastical Gothic was rising a few hundred yards away to the west. This was Gilcomston South Church at the corner of Union Street and Summer Street, designed by William Smith, the architect of Balmoral Castle. It too is of freestone and it is a fact that the contrast with the granite ashlar all around helps to underline its difference of function. It was opened in 1868.

Westward of this point most of the Union Street frontages are of two storeys but there is one notable exception. The block No. 478-484, west of Rose Street, four storeys high, stands out conspicuously.

This unusual building with pillars of the giant anta order between the first and third storeys, a channelled ground floor and surmounted by a block pediment was designed in 1830 by the city architect John Smith as the Union Street Cistern, part of the original town water supply. It was reconstructed for its present office and commercial use in 1900.

At its western end Union Street culminates in one more notable church building, St. James's Episcopal Church at the corner of Holburn Street. In pink granite of a Gothic style St. James's dates from 1887. The somewhat unfinished look about its tower is due to the fact that the plans called for a spire that was never in fact built.

It is impossible to leave the story of Union Street without some reference to one more ecclesiastical structure which though not actually on the street itself closes the view of it looking west. This is Christ's College, the original Free Church College of Aberdeen, opened in 1850 in Alford Place, the street leading west from the Union Street - Holburn Street junction — known to all Aberdonians as Holburn Junction and sometimes also as "Babbie Law", though these names are nowhere officially recognised by street signs.

Babbie Law was a real person. Her address during a large part of the nineteenth century was No. 8 Wellington Place, now a part of Holburn Street, and she was such a kenspeckle figure that she gave her name to the whole locality. She "kept a bit shoppie up stane steppies three" and was, we are told, entirely free "baith o' pride and o' malice".

> Her word was her bond, for she niffer't nae less
> > Shoppie weel stocket,
> > Door seldom locket,
> A knock brocht her ben to reopen wi' ease.

She stands as a symbol of the pleasantest aspect of byegone days in Aberdeen. She would have been startled and perhaps shocked by the rush-hour traffic glut in the vicinity of her old haunts. The homely village atmosphere in the west end of Aberdeen has gone, and she would regret that, but not everything that is new would she condemn.

Certainly she always had a soft spot for the dashing young students of Divinity who first inhabited the Free Kirk College, which in its turn became dubbed "Babbie Law".

This Tudor Gothic pile with a square tower and circular battlemented turret was designed by William Henderson. Across the way on the north side of Alford Place the beautiful library and chapel of Christ's College was built in 1887 on the site of an earlier college extension. Both this and the main Christ's College building are still in use by candidates for the ministry of the Church of Scotland.

It is impossible to forget that for eleven years — from 1870 to 1881 — the Chair of Hebrew at the college was held by William Robertson Smith, the victim of the most notorious heresy hunt in the annals of modern theology. Because of articles which he wrote for the "Encyclopaedia Britannica", on lines which scholarship has since entirely vindicated, he was removed from his chair by the Free Church General Assembly of 1881.

Posterity has made what amends it could. His centenary was celebrated at Christ's College and his portrait is perhaps the finest that hangs in the Presbytery Room there today.

Above: BON ACCORD SQUARE
Below: CHRIST'S COLLEGE, Holburn Junction

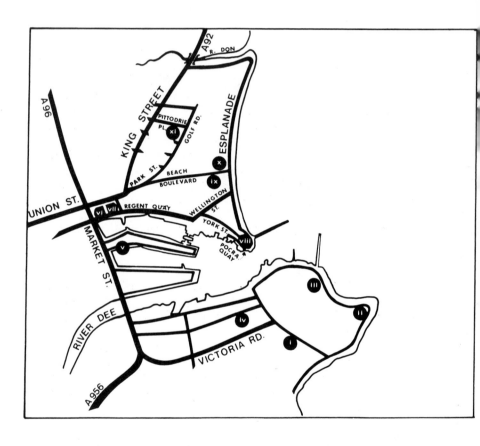

This Map covers Chapter IV (pages 73-87)

THE ITEMS OF INTEREST DO NOT NECESSARILY FOLLOW THE EDITORIAL ORDER.

I	St. Fittick's Church	VII	Old Customs House
II	Girdleness Lighthouse	VIII	Footdee Village
III	Torry Battery	IX	Pleasure Fair
IV	Marine Laboratory	X	Beach Ballroom
V	Fish Market	XI	Pittodrie Stadium
VI	Harbour Office		

CHAPTER IV — THE SEA GATES OF ABERDEEN

"And what should they know of England who only England know?"
That was the way Kipling put it. It might also be said that one cannot
know Aberdeen until one knows its setting, its hinterland and its natural
bounds. It is not merely the "fair city of the rivers twain", it is a city of the
hills and the sea. As a local poet, Marion Angus, expressed it:

> Yonder she sits beside the tranquil Dee,
> Kindly yet cold, respectable and wise,
> Sharp-tongued, though civil, with wide open eyes
> Dreaming of hills, yet urgent for the sea.

There are five bus services which carry the people of Aberdeen and
their holiday guests to the sea-gates of the city: No. 1, Garthdee to
Balgownie, traverses the entire length of Union Street passes through the
western half of the Castlegate, and turns north along King Street to the
modern Bridge of Don, where if one alights, one may walk seaward along
the two-miles-long Beach Promenade, all the way to Footdee at the other
end of the great sandy bay that is Aberdeen Beach. No. 11, Craigiebuckler
to Golf Links, also runs the entire length of Union Street and thence by
Castle Street, Justice Street, Park Street and Park Road to a terminus in
Golf Road, opposite the King's Links, a civic golf course in the grassy
hollow between the built-up area and the ridge of dunes on top of which
the Beach Promenade runs.

No. 4, Hazlehead to Sea Beach, is the most direct route of all, also
traversing Union Street and Castle Street, but cutting directly through
from Justice Street to the centre of the Beach Promenade and the Bathing
Station via the Beach Boulevard. This is the way one goes if one wants to
reach the sands with the least delay.

No. 13, Scatterburn to Footdee, carries one through the ancient
Shorelands of the city via Justice Street, Commerce Street, Castle Terrace,
Miller Street, St. Clement Street and York Street to the southern end of
the Beach Promenade and the 'back door' of the unique little Squares of
Footdee and the base of the North Pier.

But there is yet another way to reach the sea-coast and this is perhaps
the best of all if one seeks a vantage point from which to grasp with a
single sweep of the eye the sea gates of Aberdeen and their historic and
economic significance.

No. 10, the Springhill to Torry service runs along Union Terrace,
crossing Union Street at the Bridge Street - Union Terrace intersection
and proceeds thence via Bridge Street, Guild Street, Market Street,
Victoria Bridge and Victoria Road to a terminus on St. Fitticks Road,
at the base of the headland of Girdleness. It is high on this grassy peninsula
partly occupied by the Balnagask Golf Course, that one can obtain, not
merely one of the finest possible views of the city of Aberdeen, but also a
key to its strategic importance and its long maritime history.

The headland is entirely circumscribed by a promenade called Greyhope Road which hugs the seafront of the Navigation Channel, a small but historic inlet called Greyhope Bay, and then turns at first due east and then south to skirt the seaward side of Girdleness Lighthouse and enter the Bay of Nigg, a small sandy inlet in the great cliff wall that resumes its jagged sway from Gregness southward along the Kincardine coast to Stonehaven and beyond.

From Greyhope Road itself, or from various points on the higher land behind it, one may see the Harbour of Aberdeen and the towers and spires of the city laid out almost as on a map. Due north, across the slender finger of the North Pier stretch sands, links and dunes as far as the eye can reach, with the mouth of the River Dee and the Navigation Channel almost at one's feet.

We are accustomed to think of Aberdeen Bay as the two-mile crescent of sands between the rivers Dee and Don at their mouths, but this is not how the geographers look at it. Professor J. A. Steers of Cambridge in his classic description of the coastline of Scotland remarks: "From the Sands of Forvie in the north to Girdleness in the south, Aberdeen Bay is 13 miles wide and forms one of the longest stretches of lowland beach and dune coastlines in Highland Scotland. The bay has a wide radius of curvature and faces east-south-east. Three major rivers, the Dee, Don and Ythan drain the extensive hinterland of this distinctive coastline. Although the estuary of the Dee is now occupied by docks, wharves, seawalls and piers, it once had the same estuarine form as the Don and the Ythan. Each estuary had a broad tidal basin which is preceded by a gorge section. Broad sandpits seal these tidal pools, and the rivers break through to the sea through constricted channels."

Nor is that all. With one significant exception wide open beaches backed by dunes and comparatively flat inland country behind them come to a dead end at Girdleness. From the mouth of the Dee to Stonehaven the crystaline rocks of the Highland plateau form a line of cliffs of considerable variety and beauty. The one gap in this cliff wall is a little valley called the Vale of Tullos. Look to the right or south when you get off the bus at the top of St. Fittick's Road and you will see the seaward end of this vale running down to the Bay of Nigg. The landward end of it begins on the bank of the River Dee east of the hill of Kincorth a little above the railway viaduct, and it is believed that millenia ago the Dee flowed along this gap and entered the sea at the Bay of Nigg. Borings made in 1869 showed that this hollow was floored by waterborne materials and that the rock beneath them at no point rose above sea level.

It was doubtless the dramatic consequences of the Ice Age that finally changed the course of the river and caused it to flow north-east instead of south-east, forcing its way through the rock of Craiglug and flooding out into the great shallow lagoon, washing the base of the Castle Hill, that became the early harbour of Aberdeen.

In recent years the whole appearance of the Vale of Tullos has been transformed. In historic times it was a "little glen full of quiet charm." It acquired two parish churches — first the ancient parish church of St. Fittick, dedicated by Bishop David de Bernham in 1242 which still stands in ruin a little to the right of St. Fittick's Road as it gently descends to the Bay of Nigg — and the Kirk of Nigg built to replace it on the northern slope of Tullos Hill in 1829:

> No fortress guards the little vale
> Between the ocean and the Dee,
> A church its castle on the hill,
> A church its bulwark by the sea.

Still to be traced in the fabric of the St. Fittick's ruin is the outline of a former 'leper window' through which these outcasts of the middle ages were permitted to watch services. Richard Maitland, minister of Nigg from 1674 to 1715 was deposed for praying for the Old Pretender in the 1715 Rebellion. His strongly Presbyterian successor, James Farquhar, is said to have been chosen by the Presbytery for his great physical strength, which he soon showed in countering opposition to his induction. He arrived at the kirk to find two episcopalian-minded opponents beating the bellman who was trying to summon the people to worship. He tackled them both, and after knocking their heads together, strode into the church, telling the folk that if they followed him they would hear an announcement such as they had never heard before.

Generations of Aberdonians crossed the Vale of Tullos en route to Tullos Hill, the last outlier of the dwindling Grampians as they run out to the North Sea at Gregness south of the Bay of Nigg. It was, we are told, "a miniature mountain chain in itself, studded with the hillocks which are its outliers and cairns which are its peaks, with for tarns and lochs little water-filled hollows choked with water sedge and cinquefoil and carpeted around their swampy margins with the green and crimson plush of bogmoss and sundew, a carpet spangled with the orange stars of the bog asphodel".

Who enjoys this natural pageant now? Answer — the children of Tullos School. They are only half a mile away from Tullos Hill. They can still savour the moorland where heather and whin blaze in bloom of gold in spring, dark green and purple in the autumn, and there is still at Tullos an attenuated strip of woodland "that still divides the desert from the sown." But the greater part of the Vale of Tullos has been overspread with housing and with the major industrial estate developed there since the end of World War II and now throbbing with North Sea oil-related industries.

The Hill of Torry which forms the eastern and northern boundary of the Vale of Tullos became a major southern extension of Aberdeen in the years between 1881 (when it was linked to the city across the Dee by the building of Victoria Bridge) and 1900.

Established 1877

The business now carried on by John Fleming & Co. Ltd. was established in 1877 when Mr. John Fleming first came from Dundee to Aberdeen to sell timber. His first venture in the city was a success as he had chartered a sailing ship with a small cargo of White Pine from Gothenburg and disposed of it all by auction in one afternoon. Gradually an Aberdeen connection was built up, a yard was rented, and small shipments were brought in regularly over the next few years until 1885 the Albert Sawmills were opened covering a large area of Harbour land between the River Dee and Albert Basin: this area was later extended along North Esplanade West.

The latter years of the 19th century were intensively busy years for Aberdeen and to maintain supplies to the housebuilding, shipbuilding and other wood consuming trades John Fleming & Co. brought timber cargoes into Aberdeen by ship and rail from all over the world; predominantly from Scandinavia and the Russian Empire, but also from North America, while smaller quantities of exotic and expensive woods came from the Far East. In order to handle this increased volume of business the Company bought in 1901 the St. Clement's Lands in Footdee (formerly owned by the well known Aberdeen firm of Blaikie Bros.) and on this extensive area, which has been added to over the years, were built the offices and sawmills which exist today.

The Mr. John Fleming who first came as a young man to Aberdeen in 1877 settled permanently in the city soon afterwards and in course of time became well known to his fellow citizens as Sir John Fleming, Lord Provost from 1898 to 1902 and thereafter Liberal Member of Parliament for South Aberdeen. His grandson is chairman of the Company today.

John Fleming & Co. Ltd. continues to be active in business in Aberdeen and in the last few years has to set itself on a course of systematic expansion throughout Scotland. In 1959 the Company acquired its main Aberdeen competitor George Gordon & Co. Ltd. with property on Blaikie's Quay and in subsequent years has established a comprehensive trading centre in the Bridge of Don Industrial Estate. It now owns sawmills and timber yards not only in Aberdeen but in Elgin, Inverness, Glasgow, Grangemouth and Lerwick. The Head Office of this large and growing organisation remains in Baltic Place, Aberdeen.

John Fleming & Company Ltd.

Fleming

Timber Importers & Sawmillers

BALTIC PLACE, ABERDEEN.   TEL. 55443

ALSO AT ELGIN, INVERNESS, GLASGOW, GRANGEMOUTH & LERWICK

Above: TORRY POINT BATTERY and Below
PART OF ABERDEEN HARBOUR

But to return to the peninsula of Girdleness. The lighthouse at the tip of the headland was built in 1832-33. Its designer was Robert Stevenson, the grandfather of Robert Louis Stevenson. Attached to it were ten acres of grazing land 'to provide cows grazing for each of the light keepers'. Eight acres of this grazing land — no longer needed for the light keepers' cows — were purchased in 1901 by Aberdeen Town Council to form Torry's first and only public park — the Walker Park.

Another structure on the green headland, the Torry Fort, was built in 1860 and equipped with 60-pounder guns which at the time were considered to be 'quite warlike' but by the end of the nineteenth century it was 'doubted if the Fort would be of much use owing to the vast improvement of the armament of ships of war'. Nevertheless in two world wars the strategic significance of the heights of Girdleness were recognised and systems of dugouts were dug on the summit. Today the old fort is a pleasant viewpoint and its massive arched entrance gateway surmounted by a lintel with large lettering announcing 'Torry Point Battery' is an interesting architectural survival. In the open centre of the fort is a new flagstaff gifted by Junior Chamber Aberdeen in 1972.

Looking down from the heights of Girdleness towards the west and the north-west, one sees today the three tongues of neatly squared off water which form the present-day harbour of Aberdeen. The nearest of these tongues (from this viewpoint) is the River Dee, which with its weight of water from the corries of the distant Cairngorms, assisted by constant dredging, scours out the harbour entrance and makes it fit to receive its sea-borne traffic.

Never was that traffic more copious than today, for in the past decade there has been added to the long procession of diesel trawlers, whose annual freight of £26,000,000 worth of fish maintains the output of the third fishing port in Britain, and to the cargoes of freighters from the Seven Seas, the host of oil-rig supply craft that service North Sea oil-fields anything up to 200 miles offshore.

As Professor Steers indicated in the quotation on a previous page, all this is a man-made landscape. Looking down 200 years ago from the same viewpoint one would have seen an almost landlocked lagoon, a wide shallow basin of water, which at low tide became a sandy delta. Originally the narrow entrance channel to the open sea was obstructed by shoals and sandbanks and by a large awkward chunk of rock called Knock Metellan. In 1610 this obstacle was removed by David Anderson of Finzeach. At low tide he attached a string of empty casks to the offending rock, and when the tide came in he was able to lift it from its bed, and with the aid of the casks to tow it away—all for an inclusive fee of 300 merks. This feat earned him the sobriquet of 'Davie Do A'thing'.

Where the North Pier projects today from the southern end of Aberdeen Bay there was a sandbank called the Sandness. Between 1769 and 1780 this was replaced by a pier 1,200 feet long, designed by John Smeaton. Telford extended it by 900 feet in 1810-16 and a final 500 feet were added in 1874-79. Between 1869 and 1873, a new channel was excavated for the River Dee, enabling a large part of the harbour to be reclaimed. The reclaimed land was then laid out with streets and provided with sites for industrial use.

The marvel is, that from the thirteenth century, and despite all the defects of its natural harbour, Aberdeen was in the forefront of Scotland's trade with the continent of Europe. Beginning with the original commercial export of salmon, an important trade developed with Flanders in wool, cloth, hides and skins. Trade with the Baltic followed in the fifteenth century and close links were established with Danzig, while, in the Netherlands, Campvere, the Scottish Staple or clearing-house of continental trade loomed large. In 1685, Sir Patrick Drummond, Conservator of Scottish privileges on the continent reported that Aberdeen at that time, brought more money into Scotland than all its other burghs.

Inshore fishing was pursued from two small villages on either side of the estuary—Futty or Fittie on the north bank, and Old Torry on the south. These ancient fishing communities, though greatly altered in site and appearance, survived down to the present century, and while Old Torry has now been demolished and replaced by an oil-rig servicing depot, Fittie (or Footdee as it came to be called) has survived and will be described in due course. The doomed part of Old Torry was in fact largely built about 1850, and its loss need not be too sorely lamented, for, just a street or two away, there still survives in Abbey Road (which can be reached by turning down Abbey Place, on the north side of Victoria Road, along which the No. 10 bus runs)—a charming fisher square built in 1870.

Along the south bank of the Dee as one moves westward from the river's mouth, are three important institutions: the Unilever factory in Greyhope Road, which occupies premises first tenanted by the wartime Ministry of Food, the Torry Research Station of the Department of Scientific and Industrial research and the Marine Laboratory of the Scottish Department of Agriculture and Fisheries. Each performs an inter-related function. The Marine Laboratory studies the fish in their own element and the means of locating and catching them. The Research Station studies how fish can best be preserved, processed and prepared as food and kept in the pink of condition for human consumption. Unilever convert the know-how made available by the government scientists, utilising and perfecting techniques of accelerated freeze-drying and other methods.

The Marine Laboratory has its own fleet of research vessels, and advises the government on the conservation of fish stocks in the northern half of the North Sea. It follows the migration of the herring shoals and the plankton upon which they feed, and it carries out long-term experiments on fish farming. The largest of its research vessels, the 190 ft. Explorer, with its three large laboratories and delicate recording instruments—load meters, spread meters and underwater cameras—provides a set of data on the load carried by trawl warps, the spread of the wings of the trawl and other details necessary to build up a picture of the trawl in action.

All this is of intense relevance to the present-day fishing community in modern Torry, for just at the precise period when the building of Victoria Bridge opened up a great southward extension of Aberdeen, a maritime revolution transformed the economic life of the city. In 1882, a few local businessmen formed a syndicate and acquired a steam tug-boat called the **Toiler**, "for the purpose of prosecuting trawl fishing". After six months the syndicate paid out a dividend of 100%. Line fishing from scores of little havens around the coasts of north-eastern Scotland reacted to the shock-wave of the new method. Fisher families from these tiny ports flooded into Aberdeen, and in particular to the new suburb of Torry, where they were joined by business men from the English ports, anxious to participate in the Aberdeen trawling boom. The Albert Basin, the second of the tongues of water created by the new harbour works— the one between the River Dee and the commercial docks farther north, became the base of Aberdeen's new trawler fleet.

A fish market was built around the upper end of the Albert Basin in 1889, and in 20 years, the number of trawlers had risen to 205, and about 25,000 people ashore and afloat were dependent on the new industry. Today, a visit to the Fish Market is still one of the unforgettable experiences which any visitor to Aberdeen should on no account miss. As it happens, it lies on the route of the No. 10 bus in Market Street, and the visit should be paid if possible around 8 a.m. Despite the introduction of some catch-disposal by contract, the vast bulk of the daily fish landings is sold by auction, and this provides a highly colourful spectacle. To the bystander, the thrill of seeing merchanting firms compete for the fish is invariably a memorable one. A new fish market is being created simultaneously with the other great improvements at the harbour necessitated by the North Sea oil boom. Nearby is berthed the St. Clair, the new P. & O. roll-on-roll-off ferry to Lerwick in Shetland.

Thanks to the oil boom, over £15 million of public and private investment has been committed to developments in the Aberdeen harbour area since 1972. The conversion of the two former enclosed basins, Victoria Dock and the Upper Dock, to full 24-hour tidal working at a cost of £3 million was a crucial factor. Over 20 oil rigs in the North Sea are being serviced from Aberdeen, and the port now has six major oil-exploration servicing bases. Support bases for their own exclusive use have been established by Amoco, Shell, Texaco and Total. Amoco is on the Footdee side of the harbour at Pocra Quay. Texaco, Shell and Total are on the River Dee in the area of Old Torry, and there, too, at Maitland's Quay West is the Aberdeen Wood Group, who with Seaforth Maritime's Seabase—at Waterloo Quay East—are providing 'non-stop-shop', for services offered by Aberdeen commercial service companies.

FOOTDEE AND THE SHIPYARDS

To see the other half of Aberdeen's harbour quarter, it is a good plan to use the No. 13 bus from Scatterburn to Footdee. After a journey through the St. Clements industrial area, this will drop you at the southern end of the Aberdeen Bay and Beach Promenade, just at the thresh-hold of the Squares of Footdee, which constitute Aberdeen's Conservation Area No. 6.

Footdee is the home of a very ancient fisher community, which for centuries lived quite apart from the burgh of Aberdeen. Two hundred years ago, Fittie or Futty (for nobody would have called it Footdee then) consisted of "several rows of low thatched cottages running from east to west between the high road and the harbour, or as it was called 'the Tide' which at high water came even up to the walls of the houses". This was the description of a young girl who lived there at the time of the American War of Independence. She knew the old "fish town" when it was sited much further west than at present, before the wonderful efflorescence of Aberdeen shipbuilding skill which produced the Aberdeen Clipper.

But at the beginning of the nineteenth century, the Town Council of Aberdeen, to make way for harbour development, pulled down the old thatched hovels and rebuilt Footdee behind the old Blockhouse at the base of the North Pier. It was a "model village", designed by John Smith, City Architect of Aberdeen, built in the years 1808 and 1809 and consisting of two squares, called North and South Squares, to which Middle Row in South Square and Pilot's Square were added later. All the houses were originally single-storey but-and-ben cottages. This may sound rather primitive, but the houses which John Smith built were good solid structures and happily most of them have survived to the present day, still largely inhabited by the old fishing stock. Aberdeen Town Council sold them to their occupiers in 1880, and there was considerable independent rebuilding after that.

It is, however, an interesting and gratifying thing, that all major development of Footdee has been carried out by Aberdeen Town Council. John Smith added four houses to the original scheme in 1837. The Footdee Mission Hall was added in 1869, and a spate of activity took place in 1870, all by William Smith, son of John. This included the rebuilding of the old "school" in North Square, now two-storey four-roomed dwelling houses, three houses on the east side of Pilot's Square and, in 1873, three more houses on the west side of Pilot's Square.

By the middle of this century, pressure to convert these old houses and equip them with fully modern amenities became acute. There was a danger that if these conversions were carried out piecemeal by individual proprietors, the whole character of the scheme would be ruined. Again Aberdeen Town Council stepped in. The City Architect drew up comprehensive plans showing how conversions could be carried out which retained the unique old-world character of Footdee. In 1970, an exhibition was staged, at which, by means of a model and plans, the approved types of conversions were demonstrated. It was estimated that the improvements would probably cost around £1,000 per house, for which the grant aid, amounting to half the cost would be available. In addition, the council undertook to improve the roads, and lay-out and landscape the squares so as to allow for garden space, paving, drying facilities and outhouses. They also undertook to provide car parks at the back of the squares, and, on the sea-front of Aberdeen Bay, a children's playground with "adventure" features.

Nobody who takes a look at the pleasant amenity area at the back of South Square facing the sea, where old lifeboat sheds have been cleared away and the gleaming white annexes—by which these old houses have been supplied with modern bathroom and kitchen accommodation—make an unobtrusive uniform line, can regret these improvements.

Over the past half century, Footdee has become a favourite resort of summer visitors. In the Third Statistical Account of Aberdeen, Hugh Mackenzie summed up its attraction in these words: "Its isolated position, its secluded atmosphere and the unexpected cleanliness of the squares are a never failing attraction to the city-dweller. These, however, are only the outward marks of another quality which is difficult to define, but which leaves a lasting impression. The visitor to Footdee, if he lingers, takes away with him an impression, not only of its seclusion and its cleanliness, but also of its independence, its courage, its religious fervour . . . an unusual and remarkably compact village community which finds itself within the boundary of a modern city."

In Footdee there are still old folk who were born and bred there in a tightly knit patriarchal inshore fishing community in which the women-folk were of vital importance to the workaday way of life. Who can forget the song of the Footdee fisherwife:

> We brak nae breid o' idlecy
> Doon-bye in Fittie Square,
> A' nicht oor men toil on the sea
> An' wives maun dae their share.

> Sae fan the boats come laden in,
> I tak my fish tae toon,
> An' comin' back wi' empty creel
> Tae bait the lines sit doon.

> Fa wid be a fisherman's wife
> Tae run wi' the creel, the scrubber an' the knife?
> It's a doon-ruggin' life
> An' it's up tae the mussels i' the mornin'.

From the Footdee Squares, one emerges on the north side of the Navigation Channel at the Round House, the headquarters of the pilotage service, built in 1858 to give an uninterrupted view of Aberdeen Bay and the coast beyond it as far north as Buchan-ness. Pocra Quay, immediately to the west, is now a main berthing place of the North Sea oil industry supply vessels, and Footdee itself is now virtually hemmed in by North Sea oil support bases.

Still farther west is the shipbuilding yard of Hall Russell and Company, which now operates as a joint unit with the historic firm of A. Hall and Company, giving employment to about 1,220 Aberdeen and Footdee folk. It was here that there was born the family of craft which revolutionised transport by sea in the great days of the sail—the Aberdeen Clippers. They were the invention of Alexander Hall, whose initiative in designing a sailing ship cunningly tapered at the bows, the **Scottish Maid,** revealed the potentialities for speed of the type, and in the 1850's, vessels like the **Stornoway** and the **Chrysolite** pioneered British ascendancy in the race to China for tea. After 1852, Aberdeen shipbuilders turned out many fine clippers for the China run, and also for cargo and passenger trade with Australia and South Africa. In the 1860's, classic models like the **Flying Spur, Yangtse, Black Prince** and **Jerusalem** were the envy of all sailing ship men, and **Thermopylae,** racing the Clyde-built **Cutty Sark** demonstrated that she was the fastest clipper in the world.

The opening of the Suez Canal in 1869 marked the end of the great clipper ship era, but the Aberdeen shipyards continued to boom, and as late as 1890, they turned out 15 ships of 9,288 tons and employed over 2,500 men. Today Hall, Russells and the other Aberdeen yard, John Lewis and Sons of Torry, build a great range of craft from large trawlers to tugs and car and passenger ferries.

Aberdeen's commercial shipping is concentrated in the Victoria and Upper Docks. There are regular freight services from the West European ports from Dunkirk to Ghent, and from the Scandinavian ports as far as Helsinki and Abo, as well as from Canada and Portugal. The visitor delights to see cargoes of maize from Constanza on the Black Sea imported as farm feeding stuffs, much timber from Scandinavia and fertilisers from South America and from Japan.

The facade of buildings along Regent Quay is an imposing one, and includes at No. 35, a particularly attractive Georgian mansion, the Old Custom House. It was built in 1771 in the late Rennaisance style of architecture by James Gordon of Cobairdy, a returned but 'unpardoned' Jacobite who had joined Bonnie Prince Charlie at Holyrood House in 1745, and after being present at the battle of Culloden, went into exile in France. He returned to this country in 1762, and as late as 1772 was still attempting to obtain a pardon—without success.

In 1772, Gordon insured his new house on the Quay with the Sun Fire Office and, as was the custom in those days, a gilded sun cast in lead and embossed with the policy number—315283—still clearly legible after two centuries, was placed over the entrance doorway. Gordon died in his new house in May 1773, and in January 1774, his son and heir disposed of the property to "Theophilus Ogilvie, Collector of Customs at Aberdeen and his successors in Office". The building thus became Crown property, and it is still occupied by the Customs and Excise today.

The Regent Quay frontage, in hand-dressed granite ashlar from the Loanhead Quarries, has a pedimented doorway, reached by a short flight of granite steps with moulded treads. It is a superb example of well-proportioned design with carefully studied fenestration.

Farther west, at No. 16 Regent Quay, is the Harbour Office with its tower which dates from 1883 and appropriately dominates the quayside skyline.

THE SEA BEACH

For natives and visitors alike, the Sea Beach of Aberdeen is still as it has been from the earliest times, the most popular of public play areas. The great dune-fringed bay, lined by grassy links, has etched itself deep in the memory of generations of poets and exiles.

In World War II, from the Middle East, the well-known modern poet, G. S. Fraser, son of a former town clerk of the city, wrote a "Home Town Elegy" in which he recalled Aberdeen's
Night shining shop fronts, or the sleek sun flooding
The broad abundant dying sprawl of the Dee
And then he added:—
For these and for their like my thoughts are mourners
That yet shall stand though I come home no more.
Gas works, white ballroom, and the red brick baths
And salmon nets along a mile of shore,
Or beyond the municipal golf course, the moorland paths
And the country lying quiet and full of farms.
This is the shape of a land that outlasts a strategy
And is not to be taken by rhetoric and arms.

Some details of course do change. The red brick baths have gone, but the white ballroom and the 'salmon nets along a mile of shore' are still there, and the seafront itself, part of Aberdeen's window on the immensities of nature remains a phenomenon 'that outlasts a strategy'

The No. 4 bus from the city centre will deposit you at the very door of the Beach Ballroom which also offers admirable restaurant facilities. On the way you will have glimpsed the highest of those permanent dunes at the Links, the Broad Hill, a mere 94 ft. in height, but still an invigorating

Opposite:
OLD CUSTOMS HOUSE

Below:
A CORNER OF
FOOTDEE VILLAGE

viewpoint. In total the Links (where golf has been played since 1625) extend to 500 acres, the largest part of which is taken up by an 18-hole golf course, 6590 yards in length. The starting point is in Golf Road (served by the No. 11 bus) almost in the shadow of the Pittodrie football ground where Aberdeen F. C. play.

In the immediate vicinity of the Beach Ballroom are to be found children's play facilities, arranged in simulation of a North-east fishing village with harbour and boats, a railway station and railway line, and fishing nets hanging up to dry. It is the most attractive of the city's playgrounds and thousands of children use it every day during the summer.

Nearby is a large flat open space on which people can picnic or play games, and which at certain seasons of the year is used for cricket or for hockey. To the north there is a crazy golf course, a putting green, outdoor table tennis and a nine-hole pitch and putt course. In 1970 there opened, on the south of the Beach Boulevard, a large new funfair, a quarter of which is under cover.

The two miles of sand between Don and Dee have, down the centuries, provided at various times, civic sports from archery to horse racing. For a very long time now, however, they have been sacred to the normal family pleasures of the seaside: bathing, (in areas specially designated for this) picnicking, sand castle building and all the other delights of a sandy beach for the young of all ages.

It would be nice to say that the beach has remained unchanged and never under threat, but this is not quite true. In the 1960's Aberdeen became aware that it was subject to dangerous erosion and the Corporation undertook a scheme of coast protection, costing over £1 million.

A report by a London firm of consulting engineers revealed that the profile of the beach throughout its length had altered in an alarming degree over a half a century. In 1907 it rose, from the high water mark to the summit of the dunes which carry the Beach Promenade, at a gradient of one in 51. By 1960, this gradient had steepened to one in 25.

The Corporation was warned that if unchecked, this erosion would ultimately destroy the unprotected dunes so that the road around the golf links (the Beach. Promenade) would have to be abandoned and the invading Spring tides would lap the city.

Pointing out that Aberdeen Bay was exposed south-east to north-east to a stretch of the North Sea roughly 400 miles from the coast of Europe, and to waves 16 feet in height with a length of 320 feet, the experts showed that the erosion could be countered by exploiting the northerly littoral drift, which is a feature of the entire coastline. By a system of groynes at frequent intervals along the seafront, the sand and gravel being removed by the attacking waves and borne northward, could be trapped and retained to compensate for loss of this material. In order to prevent the groynes being outflanked, however, the natural "green wall" of the dunes would have to be reinforced by revetments throughout the whole length of the seafront.

In the years that followed, this prescription was adopted. The groynes were laid down and linked by revetments of pre-cast concrete blocks set in panels, and a pre-cast coping with promenade walk was laid down half way up the dunes. In this way, Aberdeen—as it has so often done in the past—made a virtue of necessity, providing at the same time a new amenity for its beach promenaders. The scheme proved a complete success. The Beach, and the Links behind, was saved for the present—and for posterity.

The effect of the still continuing northerly littoral drift can be seen in dramatic form at the mouth of the River Don. A sandbar built up from the south has gradually formed across the mouth of the river, forcing it to turn north for a considerable distance along the Balgownie coast before finding its exit to the open sea.

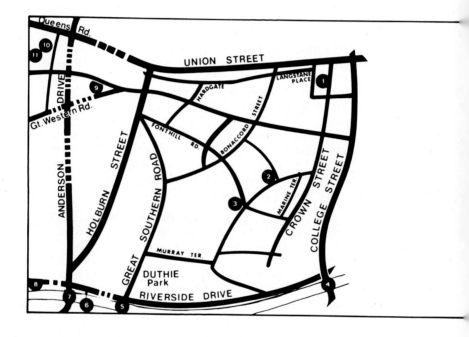

This Map covers Chapter V (pages 89-97)

THE ITEMS OF INTEREST DO NOT NECESSARILY FOLLOW THE EDITORIAL ORDER.

1 G.P.O.

2 Ferryhill North Church

3 Ferryhill South Church

4 Wellington Suspension Bridge

5 George VI Bridge

6 Ruthrieston Pack Horse Bridge

7 Bridge of Dee

8 School of Architecture and Gray's School of Art

9 Mannofield Church

10 Craigiebuckler Church

11 Macaulay Institute

CHAPTER V — THE OUTER CITY

Some two miles from the city centre, Aberdeen is encircled by an important by-pass or Ring Road extending in a wide semi-circle from the Bridge of Dee in the south, to the former burgh of Woodside in the north. Named Anderson Drive, after Sir Alexander Anderson, a great Victorian entrepeneur and Lord Provost of the city, this motorway, centred for long stretches by beds of roses, acts like the rim of a wheel from which all the main spokes converge, either directly or indirectly upon Union Street.

The area west of Anderson Drive is almost wholly of post-war development. When moving westward, therefore, along any of the spokes of the wheel from its hub at the city centre, one may trace in ever-widening circles, the change from the solid granite tenements and stately villas of the Victorian age to the genteel granite-faced bungalows of the period between the two world wars, and then discover in the outer circle, so to speak, the major housing areas of Kincorth, Garthdee, Kaimhill, Airyhall, Craigiebuckler, Hazlehead, Summerhill, Mastrick and Northfield.

Public transport follows the spokes rather than the rim of the wheel. But this is a great advantage to the explorer of the city, for it enables him to take in by the way, many historic and interesting features which he would otherwise miss. Let us then move round the outer city from south to north, using the invaluable bus services. The Kincorth Circular service, Nos. 15-16, is helpful for a start. If you catch this bus moving west from the Union Street-Bridge Street intersection it will carry you down Crown Street through Ferryhill to Duthie Park and Kincorth.

Crown Street was the creation of the Hammermen's Corporation of the Seven Incorporated Trades of Aberdeen, but its style of architecture was laid down by the Town Council, who, in the year 1804, ruled that "the front houses between each opening or cross street shall form one compartment and shall be of the same height of five wall number of floors and pitch of roof and that the whole shall be of well-dressed granite stones". In addition, it was stipulated that "front walls shall be retired eight feet from each side of the street, so as to form a sunk floor or area of that breadth, having an iron railing towards the street, which will be found not only very convenient and useful, but will tend much to beautify the street itself . . ."

All this is interesting as an example of rigid town planning regulations of 175 years ago, and while sunk areas and railings may not be so popular today, at least the rigidly enforced uniformity resulted in streets that had simplicity and dignity.

The General Post Office in Crown Street, designed in the Office of Works in Edinburgh, was opened in 1907. Its flamboyant castellated style while offering a strong contrast to the simplicity of the street's domestic uniformity, does give it a salient feature. In its early days, Crown Street petered out about Springbank Terrace, and it was not until 1883 that the town council embarked on a scheme which would provide "improved access from Ferryhill to Aberdeen"—for until then, Ferryhill was a remote rural area taking its name from the Upper Ferry on the Dee, in which a few aristocratic mansions had been built in the eighteenth century. It was separated from Aberdeen by the vale of the Howe Burn and the main access to the town from the south-west was farther west along the line of the ancient Hardgate.

Modern Crown Street dips down beyond Springbank Terrace, a handsome residential street on the right, to Dee Village Road (named after a vanished hamlet) and Millburn Street, where the Aberdeen Electricity Works stand, now only office accommodation for the "Hydro Board", and passing Ferryhill North Church (built in 1877 to plans by William Smith) ascends Ferryhill Road. Architectural enthusiasts may feel it worth while at this point, to drop off and take a look at some interesting buildings in this vicinity. On the high cape of land overlooking Ferryhill North Church and the Electricity Works from the south is Marine Terrace, built in 1847 to plans by Archibald Simpson. Along with the neighbouring streets it has been designated as Aberdeen's Conservation Area No. 5. This was one of the very last schemes Simpson designed, for, as mentioned earlier, he died in that same year, and the Marine Terrace layout was never completed. As it stands however, it is a stately single-storey, basement and attic row, with a central block of two storeys.

Marine Terrace can be approached from the top of Ferryhill Road, where at its junction with Fonthill Road stands the dominating Ferryhill South Church with its lofty spire, designed by Duncan McMillan and opened in 1874. From this point, Marine Terrace can be reached by Ferryhill Place, and close by, in Devanha Gardens, is Devanha House (1840) in the characteristic classic style of Archibald Simpson. Bow ended at east and west, it has a fine four-columned fluted Doric porch with pediment, and there is an attic pediment over the second storey above.

In Bon-Accord Street nearby (first on the right along Fonthill Road) is Ferryhill House (No. 163). Now an hotel, it was built about 1780 and has an arched and keystoned centre door between handsome bow windows.

From Ferryhill South Church the No. 15/16 bus now descends to the Duthie Park on the banks of the Dee via Polmuir Road, Murray Terrace and Great Southern Road. The story of how Miss Elizabeth Crombie Duthie of Ruthrieston acquired the various lands that make up the Duthie Park and presented them to the city of Aberdeen, to be opened by Princess Beatrice on September 27, 1883 is a saga in itself. A special Act of Parliament was required to secure the compulsory purchase of the estate of Arthurseat, whose legal owner, A. S. Williamson had gone to Australia and disappeared from mortal ken.

Miss Duthie is commemorated in the park by a statue of Hygeia, the goddess of health, atop a lofty fluted column with Corinthian capital guarded by four decorative lions. The park with its cricket fields, model

Opposite:
THE GENERAL POST
OFFICE, CROWN ST.

Below:
MARINE TERRACE
an incomplete classical
Archibald Simpson
terrace

yachting pond, duck and children's boating lake and ever-colourful flower-beds is 42 acres in extent. The new Winter Gardens opened in 1970 replace the old conservatory dating from 1891 and provide a superb focal feature. Constructed largely of glass and aluminium they comprise a large conservatory 50 yards long connected to a series of greenhouses and courtyards through which the public can wander at will. Alongside is a new restaurant with seating capacity for 100 with full dining facilities.

In the courtyard of the new gardens are displayed with admirable art and pleasing design a whole range of relics from the discarded past of the city — Kelly's Cats from Union Bridge, bygone Provost's lamps, stately Victorian lamps from Victoria Park and perhaps most intriguing of all, Alex. Fidler's horse trough which originally stood in Guild Street, with its eccentric inscription:

> Water springs for man and beast,
> Your service I am here,
> Although six thousand years of age
> I am caller, clean and clear . . .

And then that triumphant touch of unlimited benevolence —
FOR THE INHABITANTS OF THE WORLD

The southern boundary of the Duthie Park runs along Riverside Drive, a delightful promenade and motorway along the left bank of the river, which runs from Victoria Bridge to the Bridge of Dee, passing on the way the charming Wellington Suspension Bridge, built in 1820, and the Railway Viaduct (1848-50) while the King George VI Bridge, opened by King George in 1941, now forms the main traffic exit from Aberdeen to the south and the main link between the city and its south bank satellite of Kincorth.

Across the handsome bridge our bus will now carry us to coast up Provost Watt Drive to Tollohill Square at the base of the 13-storey high flats tower which forms the central feature of the new community. Kincorth was the earliest of Aberdeen's post-war housing estates. It was designed on lines suggested by an international competition in 1938, though not actually implemented until the end of World War II. A large proportion of the houses are faced with granite, for it was conceived in an age when Aberdeen was still 'the Granite City' and any other material for a show-place housing scheme was unthinkable.

By the end of the Sixties Kincorth was a municipal housing estate of 3053 houses and a population of around 10,000. It had its own shopping centre, six schools, two churches, library, clinic, community centre and village green and the infrastructure was completed in 1971 with the opening of Kincorth Academy, its £1,000,000 secondary 'neighbourhood comprehensive' school.

Above: RUTHRIESTON PACK HORSE BRIDGE which carried south traffic into Aberdeen. The parapet is a modern addition for safety of pedestrians.

Below: BRIDGE OF DEE built in early 16th century.

Yet this post-World War II satellite town is not without its stirring history. Tollohill, the Hill of Kincorth, was occupied on Monday, June 16, 1639, by the Earl Marischal and his Army of the Covenant bent on reducing the refractory Royalist forces in the burgh of Aberdeen to his will. Very soon he was joined by other Covenanting forces under the Marquess of Montrose and the Earl of Kinghorne. To this day their camping ground has been known as Covenanters' Fauld. Inevitably the first streets to be laid out in Kincorth, on the slopes facing the River Dee from the south were called Covenanters Drive and Covenanters Row, to be followed by Faulds Gate and Faulds Wynd.

On June 17th and 18th the Covenanters descended from their 'fauld' and engaged in decisive battle at the Bridge of Dee immediately below with the Royalist army led by the Earl of Aboyne supported by the loyal citizens of Aberdeen. The opposing forces were roughly equal on both sides with about 2500 men taking part on each — except for the artillery. The defenders brought to the bridge 'four brass pieces qhuilk did little skaith' while the Covenanters brought into play their 'fearful cartow' a weapon which did frightful damage.

All Tuesday the battle raged and despite the Covenanters' cannon the defenders did not yield. The crisis was reached the next day when fifty of the defending musketeers left the scene to bury a dead comrade. At the same time the Covenanters carried out a wily feint by sending 200 men upstream as if to ford it at a higher point. Lord Aboyne then left fifty men to defend the bridge and went off to intercept the outflanking manoeuvre. The assault on the bridge was renewed with redoubled violence. This time it succeeded. The defence turned into a rout and the way to Aberdeen lay open.

From the heights of Kincorth one looks directly down on the ancient Bridge of Dee which yet stands as one of the great medieval monuments of the city. It will repay a closer look.

When built between 1520 and 1527 by Bishop Gavin Dunbar it was unique among Scottish bridges of that time. There were seven semi-circular ribbed arches. Instead of rising to a peak in the middle the roadway and arches were level, which was not customary, and above each pier was a recess from the roadway for the added safety of foot passengers. The bridge also had, and still has today, an unprecedented array of coats of arms and commemorative inscriptions carved upon it: the arms of Scotland, of the Regent Albany, of Bishop Elphinstone and of Bishop Dunbar himself. In addition a chapel for wayfarers and a great protective port or gateway were built at the south end. These additional features have gone but the bridge itself has been little altered down 400 years. It was widened in 1841-2.

Assuming we have reached the Bridge by walking down from the Kincorth civic centre let us now cross it. Turning east a little way along

Riverside Drive on the river's left bank we may examine another very old but much smaller bridge which stands on the strip of parkland between the motorway and the river.

This is the old Ruthrieston pack horse bridge, a picturesque structure with three arches and squat buttresses, built in 1693-4 by Aberdeen Town Council to carry the old highway from the Bridge of Dee over the Ruthrieston Burn and northward into the town by the Hardgate. It has been supplied with a parapet for the safety of pedestrians, but originally it had none, since the bulky packs carried by the pack horses would have projected over the width of the bridge.

We are now in the Ruthrieston area of the city. Ruthrieston is a corruption of Ruadri's Town a very ancient settlement taking its name from Ruadri, the Celtic mormaer or Earl of Mar in the early twelfth century who had a motte or timber and earthwork stronghold in the area. This area around the Bridge of Dee has always been of great strategic importance and today it is still of special significance to Aberdonians, for here they can look across and up the river into truly rural country quite unspoilt by urban sprawl.

West of the bridge on the south side of the river A943, the South Deeside Road, after less than a mile, crosses a tiny stream at Hilldowntree, and leaving everything urban behind runs into richly wooded lands alongside the Dee in the parish of Banchory-Devenick. Here a side road to the south strikes over the watershed of the Mounth by the Blue Hill (467 ft.) with a hill indicator pinpointing Cairngorm peaks far on the west. From this upland road the view of the Deeside suburbia on the north side of the river, as one looks back towards Aberdeen, takes the breath away. It reveals seven miles of almost continuous riverside communities perched on the delta terraces above Dee's left bank — the villages of Cults, Bieldside, Murtle, Milltimber and Peterculter, all served by A93, the North Deeside Road.

The townward end of this road is served by two city bus services, No. 24 which runs from western Union Street along Holburn Street and turns west to run out of the city by Great Western Road and No. 2 which uses Broomhill Road, a parallel western artery a little farther south, also debouching from Holburn Street on the right or west. It has its terminus on the low river haughland at Garthdee where it links up with the No. 1 bus services (Balgownie - Garthdee) on the city boundary. By walking a short distance westward on Garthdee Road from this point one soon reaches the Den of Cults from which one can turn right to climb a short brae to rejoin the North Deeside Road at Cults Square. The No. 1 bus traverses the whole length of Holburn Street to the Bridge of Dee and turns right there to run along Garthdee Road parallel to the left or north bank of the river.

Between the Bridge of Dee and the city boundary at Garthdee there lies a major housing scheme embracing about 5000 people. It occupies an area about a mile long and half a mile wide and takes its name from the two farms of Kaimhill and Garthdee, which until World War II were virtually the only features of the whole area. The land itself was mostly purchased by Aberdeen Corporation in 1938 but it was not until after World War II that the major part of it was converted into streets and houses. The No. 2 and No. 1 bus services will give you a good idea of this quarter of 'new Aberdeen'. On the gloriously wooded banks of the river just opposite the Garthdee terminus are two important Aberdeen institutions — the Scott Sutherland School of Architecture, housed in an extended mansion, Garthdee House, and immediately to the west of it Gray's School of Art in a new building opened in 1966.

Some street names in the Kaimhill - Garthdee township are a reminder that the area did have a past associated with the dramatic Civil War history of Aberdeen. Two Mile Cross was the site of the Marquess of Montrose's camp before and during the Battle of the Justice Mills in 1644 and the dreadful Sack of Aberdeen that followed it. Aboyne Road and Gardens commemorate the Earl of Aboyne, son of the Marquess of Huntly who played a leading part in the struggles of that time, while Pitmedden Terrace and Road recall "Bonnie Sir John" Seton of Pitmedden who lost his life in the Battle of the Bridge of Dee.

On its way to the west the No. 24 bus service, via Great Western Road, passes through an attractive residential area mainly built up in the latter nineteenth century of solid comely granite stone. As it nears Mannofield, a one-time rural village now centred by the tall tower and spire of Mannofield Church (1882) it passes on the right the handsome eighteenth century house of Friendville, built by a Quaker family and standing in a charming garden. At the end of its run the bus turns north up Springfield Road to the post-war housing area of Airyhall, with its own attractive branch library, where exhibitions are frequently held, and its own modern school.

Beyond this lies the massive modern private enterprise housing estate of Craigiebuckler served by the No. 11 bus service. Craigiebuckler House is the home of the Macaulay Institute for Soil Research, while Craigiebuckler Church on Springfield Road (architect A. Marshall Mackenzie) which dates from 1883, has several features of interest. The three tall lancet windows in the west gable (modelled on the thirteenth century chapel of Kildrummy Castle) carry modern stained glass designs by William Wilson representing the Last Supper, the Crucifixion and the Resurrection. The church has a remarkable historic link with Aberdeen's remote past in the shape of 'Young Lowrie, a bell cast from the metal of 'Auld Lowrie' which for 525 years had hung in the great steeple of the City Kirk of St. Nicholas .

'Auld Lowrie' was the nickname of the bell called St. Lawrence, a propitiatory gift made in 1351 by Provost William Leith of Ruthrieston for his murder of one Baillie Cattanach. Although only rung on special occasions, 'Auld Lowrie' cracked and was recast in 1634, to serve again until 1874 when in a great fire the old lead-covered oaken spire crashed into the burning building carrying 'Lowrie' with it. The fragments were collected together and recast for Craigiebuckler Church.

CRAIGIEBUCKLER PARISH CHURCH

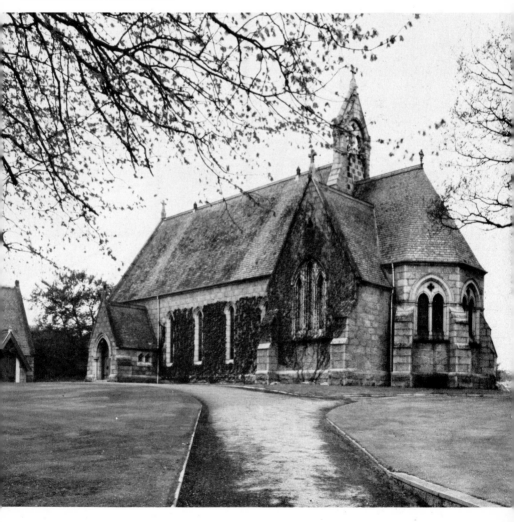

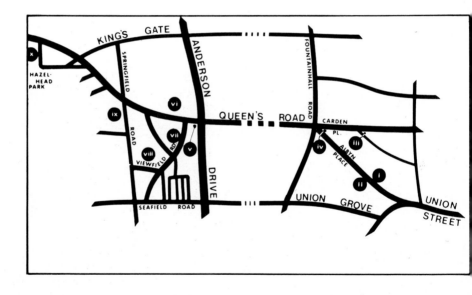

This Map covers Chapter VI (pages 99-105)

THE ITEMS OF INTEREST DO NOT NECESSARILY FOLLOW THE EDITORIAL ORDER.

I	Rubislaw Terrace Gardens	VI	Rubislaw Quarry
II	Harlaw Academy	VII	Gordons' Regimental Museum
III	St.Mary's Episcopal Church	VIII	Johnston Gardens
IV	Queen's Cross Church	IX	Walker Dam
V	School of Domestic Science	X	Hazlehead Academy

CHAPTER VI — RUBISLAW AND HAZLEHEAD

Like the west end of London, the west end of Aberdeen is now no longer an 'end', it is more like a middle. It may seem as if its solid respectable streets of Victorian villadom have over the past 70 years changed least of all in the maelstrom of modern progress. But they **are** changing and it was to keep a watchful eye on these changes that in July 1968 Aberdeen Corporation designated the Albyn Place/Rubislaw district as the city's Conservation Area No. 4. This is the area served by the No. 4 and No. 5 bus services to Woodend and Hazlehead and the No. 18 service to Summerhill.

Albyn Place, the westward continuation of Alford Place (which leads west of Holburn Junction and is served by No. 4 and 5 buses), is according to Aberdeen's Director of Town Planning "with its dignified buildings, well-kept grounds and spacious public gardens, an area of the highest amenity and a superb example of the nineteenth century design for gracious living". The streets immediately to the north of it are also very fine and contain a high proportion of listed buildings of architectural or historic interest.

Farther west still "although there are few listed buildings the architectural standard is particularly high for a residential area, and the almost universal use of finely dressed granite imparts to it a special quality not to be found in any other residential district in the world."

This area is Aberdeen's equivalent to the New Town of Edinburgh and several of its street names are due to the original ownership by James Skene of Rubislaw, a close friend of Sir Walter Scott. Victoria Street and Albert Street, both running north from Albyn Place, proclaim their origin in the first years of Victoria's reign. Waverley Place owes its name to James Skene, who illustrated so many of Sir Walter Scott's works. The early development of Albyn Place and Alford Place on the Rubislaw estate took place under the guidance of Archibald Simpson, who besides planning many 'villa residences' was also the architect of the High School for Girls (now Harlaw Academy), sometimes claimed to be in point of its noble simplicity and its superb dressed granite the finest granite building in the world. It stands a little way up Albyn Place on the south side. Facing it from the other side behind attractive public gardens is Rubislaw Terrace. This fine street was developed by Skene himself under the guidance of Simpson's artist friend James Giles, along with Simpson's architectural heirs, the firm of Mackenzie and Matthews.

It dates from 1852 and was a conscious imitation of the style of Sir Walter Scott's Abbotsford House, combining the Scottish baronial and Elizabethan styles. The plan allowed for 50 houses "alternating in pairs, the one of a superior description having handsome bow windows reaching the height of both floors with a neat balustrade, the other with plain windows." In each case the door is reached by a flight of steps — an arrangement allowed by the basement floor being half sunk.

The 'pleasure gardens' of Rubislaw Terrace, after about a century as private gardens were taken over by the town and landscaped to make one of the most beautiful open spaces in the city.

In the decade of the 1860's Carden Place, forming the third side of a triangle linking Albert Street to Albyn Place at Queen's Cross, was taking shape and here the first notable highlight was St. Mary's Episcopal Church, nicknamed 'the Tartan Kirkie' because of its variegated stonework. It was designed by Alexander Ellis in the exotic mode pioneered by William Butterfield. It dates from 1862. In 1877 John Bridgeford Pirie, Ellis's assistant, set up as an architect on his own account and many striking buildings in this part of Aberdeen bear his stamp, among them Queen's Cross Church with its towering steeple at the junction of Albyn Place and Carden Place. (Hamilton Place, which leads off Fountainhall Road and is passed by the No. 18 bus on its way to Summerhill was also a Pirie creation).

Meanwhile the No. 4 and 5 buses carry us past the Queen's Cross intersection (where a bronze statue of Queen Victoria appropriately faces west towards Balmoral) into Queen's Road, lined on both sides by the stately homes of the later nineteenth and early twentieth century. It may be of interest to note that No. 50 Queen's Road, another of Pirie's bizarre Victorian domestic villas in granite, stands on the site of Rubislaw House, which Sir George Skene had built in the second half of the seventeenth century. It had to be demolished in 1886 because it was out of alignment with the new highway.

When Queen's Road reaches the roundabout at its intersection with Anderson Drive, the ring road by-pass encircling the city, we are already sufficiently high to catch a glimpse of the sea away to the south-east, which caused this locality in byegone days to be called Bay View, and Bay View Road here at one time marked the western end of the built-up area. Today at this corner the Rubislaw playing fields of the Grammar School (now renamed Rubislaw Academy) merely mark a pause on the long processional way to the west. All the same it may be worth while to alight at this point for there are some remarkable sights in this vicinity.

Crossing Anderson Drive where the new College of Domestic Science stands at the south-west corner we may turn up Royfold Crescent on the right to reach the vicinity of the former Rubislaw Quarry.

For close on 200 years the name Rubislaw signified to the world the fine blue-grey granite extracted from this tremendous hole in the ground, a hole out of which it was proudly boasted that half of Aberdeen had come. Its dimensions were 465 feet deep, 900 feet long and 750 feet wide. It provided the stone for famous public works like Rennie's Waterloo Bridge in London and even as lately as the mid-sixties of this century the Bruce Monument at Bannockburn, Leeds University Extension, the Halls of Justice at Swindon and Dumbarton's municipal buildings. Then in 1969

ERECTED BY
THE ROYAL TRADESMEN OF ABERDEEN
1893

Things have changed a lot since 1495...

When William Elphinstone, Bishop of Aberdeen and Chancellor of Scotland founded King's College in 1495, its bell attracted scholars from all over Scotland to study the new thinking and ideas of the Renaissance as they slowly emerged from Europe.

Today, Grampian Television brings the world and its ideas every evening to homes all over the North and East.

came the shattering news that the continued working of this immense reservoir of building and decorative stone was no longer economic and would be discontinued. The days when granite could be and was used for every kind of building, domestic and public, humble and grandiose were over for ever. Returning to Queen's Road and crossing it turn down the next opening on the left (or south), Viewfield Road. A short way down on the right will be found a charming old house called St. Luke's which is now the Regimental Headquarters and museum of The Gordon Highlanders, Aberdeen's famous territorial regiment. It contains a host of interesting military byegones. St. Luke's was originally the studio of Sir George Reid, President of the Royal Scottish Academy and a very notable portrait painter. Happily the museum still includes "The Gordon's Warning" a painting which Sir George made in this same studio a century ago.

St. Luke's does not exhaust the attractions of Viewfield Road. Carry on along it and you will notice the signs pointing to Johnston Gardens, one of Aberdeen's most delightful miniature parks (with free car parking close by). Although these gardens only extend to three acres they give the impression of much greater space. Its streams, pools, rocks and waterfalls make this a beautiful place. The gardens contain collections of waterside plants, including large groups of primulas and herbaceous families, as well as rhododendrons, azaleas and an interesting collection of Alpines.

Viewfield Road, as it happens, leads eventually to Springfield Road not far from Craigiebuckler Church (already described). Just behind the church is another pleasant public open space around Walker Dam, a sheet of water that is attractive at any time of the year. It is the haunt of a family of swans for whose protection a local resident bequeathed a permanent fund. Close to the Dam is Walker Dam Infant School opened in 1966, which is famous for its two circular classrooms, the first of the kind in Scotland. The badge of the school is a white swan sailing upon the wavelets of the Dam.

Beyond Walker Dam Springfield Road reaches the western part of Queen's Road and we are within easy walking distance of Hazlehead, the great estate extending to 852 acres, of which 215 acres are woodlands. Aberdeen Town Council purchased the estate in 1920 at a cost of £40,000. Since then the magnificent public park, the golf courses and the woods, not to mention the model housing colony with its four 12-storey tower blocks amid lawns and trees, and much other municipal housing, have given the citizens a return for their investment which no one could have foreseen in these straitened days at the end of World War I. Indeed the daring of purchase in 1920 can be gauged by the letter of protest published in the local press at the time.

"It is surprising" this declared "to find such a scheme being even suggested in these fateful and highly critical times when the great bulk of people have the utmost difficulty in getting food for themselves and their children, and who are already groaning under a burden of taxation unprecedented in the history of this country".

Strangely enough in 1920 the civic fathers were buying back a part of the patrimony which they had owned 479 years previously, for Hazlehead was a part of the vast territory known as the Freedom Lands which they had received as a gift from King Robert the Bruce in 1319. When in 1551 they began to dispose of this royal gift for ready cash Hazlehead was acquired by its first private laird, Robert Chalmers, at a feu duty of £13 6s 8d. Fortunately in 1775 the estate was bought by William Rose, a native of Cromdale, who became a prominent shipowner in Aberdeen, and during the next 145 years he and successive Rose lairds lavished care and attention on the estate, adding more and more loveliness to the policies around the simple but stately house at the centre of what is now Hazlehead Park. The old mansion was replaced by a restaurant opened in 1960.

Three great redwood trees in the Park, not far from the entrance to the Zoo which is now one of its attractions, were planted to celebrate the births of successive Rose children. They now stand 93 ft., 114 ft. and 118 ft. in height and upwards of a century old, though they cannot be much older as their tribe, the Californian Giant Sequoia were only introduced into this country in 1853 and given the name Wellingtonias in honour of the Duke of Wellington.

The Park, approached by two long avenues from Queen's Road extends to over 400 acres. There are three golf courses, a putting green, a pitch and putt course, a maze, a caravan and tent site. The small Zoo aims to display a representative collection of Scottish animals. It has an attractive free-flying aviary, an excellent small aquarium, a collection of the primates and an exhibition house incorporating a lecture theatre.

Beyond the park and the well-planned Hazlehead housing estate, in Groat's Road a short distance from the city boundary, is Hazlehead Academy, the neighbourhood comprehensive secondary school for the whole area, while on the other side of the Skene Road, which takes over at this point, from Queen's Road, lies Woodend Hospital.

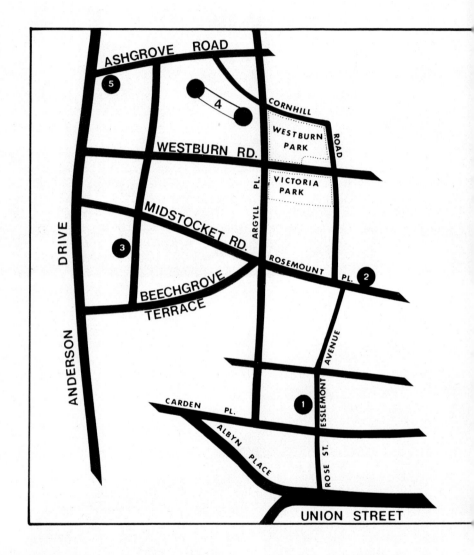

This Map covers Chapter VII (pages 107-111)

THE ITEMS OF INTEREST DO NOT NECESSARILY FOLLOW THE EDITORIAL ORDER.

1 Grammar School and Lord Byron Statue
2 Rutherford Church
3 Oakbank School
4 Aberdeen Royal Infirmary
5 Grampian Regional Headquarters

CHAPTER VII — ROSEMOUNT, MIDSTOCKET, SUMMERHILL

From a strictly geographical point of view perhaps the best way of defining South and North Aberdeen is to trace their natural dividing line along the course of that important little stream the Den Burn. Glacial ice hollowed out the ravine of that potent rivulet. Only six and a half miles long it rises on the north side of the Skene Road a little beyond the hamlet of Kingswells. It then passes exactly four miles from the Mercat Cross of Aberdeen through the Den of Maidencraig, where in 1616 the town council built what was at first called the Denburn Mill and later the Mill of Maidencraig.

This has nothing to do with a "maiden" but comes from the Gaelic word "meadhon" meaning 'middle' and refers to the steep solitary rock or 'middle craig' rising up in the dam of the mill, which was burned down in 1885, some years after which its great double wheel was sold for scrap. Half a mile farther on the Den Burn reaches Oldmill — now Woodend Hospital — the old mill being the original mill that was superseded by the Mill of Maidencraig.

At this point the stream makes two wide sweeping meanders which roughly separate the Hazlehead district from the new housing area of Summerhill. When the stream leaves Summerhill and passes under Anderson Drive (the Ring Road) it enters a beautiful piece of private parkland called Rubislaw Den, with tree-planted banks and rustic bridges. This lies between two west end residential streets, Rubislaw Den North and South whose residents use it as an amenity area. If you would like to explore this little-known pleasance it can be reached by taking the No. 18 bus up the long brae of King's Gate and alighting at Moray Place, which leads to the western end of Rubislaw Den.

The Den Burn then finds its way into the heart of Aberdeen, sometimes underground in a culvert and sometimes open to the sky in pleasant grass-fringed reaches. One of these open reaches is north of Skene Street in the grounds of the Grammar School which can be reached by alighting from the No. 18 bus at the corner of Albert Street and Carden Place and turning right down Skene Street where the Grammar School (a handsome granite building dating from 1863) will be found in its own fine grounds on the left or north side of the street. The school's most famous pupil, Lord Byron, is commemorated in a prominent statue in front of the main entrance, a notable work by the sculptor-poet, Pittendrigh MacGillivray.

The stream now flows under Esslemont Avenue but emerges again lower down (still to the north of Skene Street) in the Mackie Place Amenity Area which is in the process of re-development. Two old houses here, one with twin-shaped gables and granite ashlar frontage dating from 1810 and the other of harled brick with a shaped gable dating from 1800 are to be preserved, but the garden grounds in front, with the Den Burn flowing through them will be landscaped as part of a small public park leading east to Jack's Brae, already laid out as a sloping lawn.

At the foot of Jack's Brae the Den Burn finally disappears in a culvert and is seen no more on its subterranean journey as it coils round between the soaring 22-storey high flats of the Upper Denburn development, with its huge two-storey car park, and the Public Library, and is carried under the Schoolhill Viaduct and along the Denburn Valley and the Green to empty itself into the Upper Dock of Aberdeen Harbour.

In the lower part of Skene Street itself the south side of the street is occupied by the massive Gilcomston high flats, replacing part of the old suburb of Gilcomston. Here at Rosemount Viaduct we have arrived on the route of the No. 13 bus which serves the central part of the Rosemount area, which is also in part covered by the No.22/23 Mastrick-Northfield service. Before becoming a part of expanding Aberdeen, Rosemount, a long ridge between the Den Burn and the next stream to the north, the West Burn, was dotted with country mansions. Rosemount House, itself, which gives its name to the whole area, is a very modest two-storey granite block built before 1810 and approached from a pend in Rosemount Place. The oldest corner of the district is at the north-eastern tip where there are many listed buildings, mostly in poor condition, in Rosemount Terrace, Caroline Place, Forbes Street and Skene Square. Better preserved are some larger houses in View Terrace, Mount Street and Westburn Road.

To see the pleasantest part of Rosemount perhaps the best plan is to leave the bus at Rosemount School in Rosemount Place, a stately structure in the classical Italianate style designed by James Souttar and built in 1883-4. A little way east on the opposite side of Rosemount Place is Rutherford Church which dates from 1870. By turning north along Watson Street one reaches Victoria Park, the oldest in the city, but still one of the finest.

Laid out in 1871 on what had been a problem area to the civic fathers for many years and had been let as grazings under the name of Glennie's Parks, the Victoria Park was seen from the start as a completely new departure in civic enterprise — something shaped by man, not an inheritance from wild nature like the Links, a sort of gift of God that had belonged to the community from ancient times.

Today a feature is a Blind Garden of scented plants, with a shelter and a fountain, a rhododendron garden which provides interest in spring and early summer and collections of roses and bedding plants to continue the display throughout the year. In Victorian times it was surrounded by heavy railings but today it is open to the road and provides a beautiful view to those passing by.

The northern boundary of Victoria Park is Westburn Road, along which No. 9, No. 10 and No. 22 buses pass. Just across this main artery forming part of the city's Inner Ring Road is Westburn Park. The two areas together extend to nearly 40 acres, a virtually continuous open space

ABERDEEN ROYAL INFIRMARY COMPLEX AT FORESTERHILL and
MAIN ENTRANCE TO THE GRAMMAR SCHOOL, SHOWING STATUE OF LORD BYRON ITS MOST
FAMOUS PUPIL.

enhancing this whole district. Westburn Park contains three bowling greens, tennis courts and hockey, football and cricket pitches. Through the park runs the West or Gilcomston Burn, which has been enlarged to form a series of informal pools which attract thousands of children every summer.

Westward of the two parks, Westburn Road continues a gradual ascent through the lands that of old formed the Forest of Stocket, the royal hunting domain which King Robert I gave to the burgh as the major part of the Freedom Lands in 1319. On the right is the estate of Foresterhill which, since the 1930's has been developed as the chief hospital centre in the North of Scotland, embracing the Aberdeen Royal Infirmary, the Aberdeen University Medical School, the Royal Maternity Hospital and the Royal Aberdeen Hospital for Sick Children.

The No. 9 and 10 buses diverge here along Westburn Drive to encircle the Foresterhill complex on the north side where the main entrance lies, while the No. 13 bus reaches the western part of Westburn Road via Rosemount Place, Beechgrove Terrace and Midstocket Road, passing the two handsome churches of Beechgrove and St. Ninian's on the way. Beechgrove with its tall spire and three-lancet front in the Normandy first pointed style, was designed by George Watt and built in the period 1896-1900, while St. Ninian's with its square battlemented tower was designed by Dr. William Kelly and built in 1898. Modern vertical sundials are a comparative rarity, but the one on St. Ninian's provides a striking point of interest on a fine ecclesiastical building.

Towards the western end of Midstocket Road (No. 22/23 bus) is Oakbank School with its wide-ranging granite frontage, designed by James Matthews in 1878 as a new home for the oldest industrial school in Scotland, which had been founded by Sheriff William Watson in 1841.

West of Foresterhill, in the area below Anderson Drive is the estate of Woodhill, featuring the modern office buildings of various Grampian Regional Council departments, with, at the corner of Westburn Road and Anderson Drive, the headquarters of the Grampian Regional Council, Woodhill House.

We are here at the farthest west point on the great semi-circle formed by Anderson Drive and all around us is the new outer city created since the end of World War II. The familiar granite of the older city has disappeared save for a few decorative facings on the frontages of public buildings. But in its place is the spacious layout with generous lawns and grass verges which is characteristic of modern planning.

Opposite the end of Westburn Road, on the west side of the Ring Road, leads off the Lang Stracht, a main traffic artery leading west along

Opposite the end of Westburn Road, on the west side of the Ring Road, leads off the Lang Stracht, a main traffic artery leading west along the line of the Old Skene Road and separating the Summerhill housing estate from the huge post-war Mastrick Ward, at this southern end of which is an extensive industrial estate. The outer tip of the built-up area on the west, along the Lang Stracht, is at Sheddocksley, where the final housing colony within the former burgh boundary is being developed. It lies beyond Springhill Road, on either side of which parkland and recreation grounds have been retained.

NORTH ANDERSON DRIVE, showing some of the 100,000 rose bushes enhancing its appearance

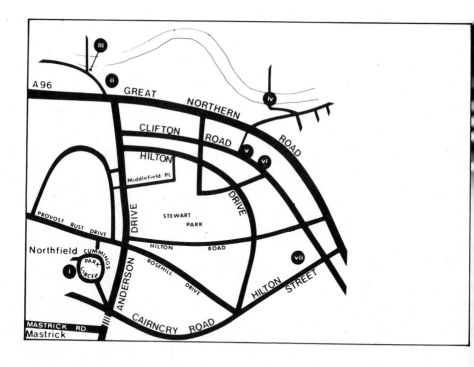

This Map covers Chapter VIII (pages 113-118)

THE ITEMS OF INTEREST DO NOT NECESSARILY FOLLOW THE EDITORIAL ORDER.

I   Post Office Tower
II   Woodside House
III "The Barracks"
IV Grandholm Works and Bridge

V   Burgh Hall
VI   Sir John Anderson Library
VII College of Education

CHAPTER VIII — MASTRICK, NORTHFIELD AND THE DON

> Towered cities please us then
> And the busy hum of men . . .

Aberdeen is now a city of many tower blocks and multi-storey flats, ranging up to 17 storeys in height but perhaps the shapeliest of them are those which cluster along the inner rim of Anderson Drive on the 'crown' of the city, the Anderson towers, Oldcroft, Buchanan, Castleton and Woodhill Courts, and the Wimpey towers, Cornhill, Rosehill and Stockethill Courts. Farther west at the centre of Mastrick there is the older Mastrick Land, a mere 14 storeys, but nothing could have exceeded the pleasure with which its first top-storey dwellers turned their eyes to the north-west and found they could easily identify the familiar outline of the Mither Tap of Bennachie from their living room windows. Others who faced to the east in blocks like Rosehill Court could see the mighty breakers rolling in to Aberdeen Bay.

The secret of the exhilaration first felt by the new population in Mastrick and Northfield, Aberdeen's greatest post-war housing estates, was in an increased contact with nature and the countryside. For there is no doubt that the Aberdonian is a countryman at heart.

No doubt the thrill wore off in time, but the proximity to open country does inspire in the visitor also a sense of going hand in hand with "the mountain nymph sweet Liberty". The 18,000-strong 'neighbourhood unit' of Mastrick, covers an area much larger than the two small farms, Mastrick and Upper Mastrick, which give the district its name. Perhaps the best way to savour it is to take the No. 23 bus which penetrates the area by Mastrick Road from Anderson Drive and, after skirting the central area with its pedestrian precinct and shopping area, goes on farther west to its terminus near Springhill Road and Regensburg Court a pleasant ten-storey housing block for old folk. It is hard to believe that it was not until 1950 that the preliminary steps were taken to develop this whole area for municipal housing, or to give it any of the five churches, ten schools and many industries and shops it has now.

The development was extremely rapid. The civic centre with its shops, library, health centre and community centre has proved a boon, but while the community is now prosperous, self-confident and well established there are calls for additional amenity of a visible kind — perhaps a civic centre garden — which would act as a strong symbol of community.

Immediately north of Mastrick, and separated from it by the long artery of Provost Fraser Drive is its neighbour Northfield. It, too, is a post-war creation though of a somewhat earlier vintage. On the Whitsunday term of 1946 the estate of Northfield, entirely farmland, was acquired by the Corporation, but its development was delayed by Government regulation until June 1949.

The Northfield neighbourhood unit, embracing the adjoining schemes Granitehill and Cummings Park was defined in the city Survey and Plan of that year. It was to cover an area of 386 acres, of which 219 acres were to be residential, providing homes for a population of 10,650. A big effort was made from the beginning to convert Northfield from a mere dormitory suburb into a living community, conscious and proud of its own identity. The Church of Scotland was there from the beginning and it was followed by the United Free Church. A combined community centre and public library was opened in 1955, the first of its kind in Scotland. History was made in the provision of houses for old folk, a residential home for the aged and an old folks' club. It was given five schools, many shops and a public house. For industry it acquired a large modern bakery and the mason's yard and joinery workshops of a big building firm.

The lands of Northfield lie on a plateau sloping down from the east and south, where Granitehill, at 420 feet above sea level, provides a site for Aberdeen's Post Office Tower on the highest point within the old burgh boundary, to the west and north, where it faces towards the Howes of Bucksburn and the valley of the Don.

Take the No. 22 bus marked Northfield (it is really the No. 23 Mastrick bus at the other end of its detour into the city centre) and it will carry you through Northfield to its terminus at Davidson Gardens. Look due west and you will see a beguiling rural view. The hill in the background is Brimmond Hill (869 ft.) which has been a resort of Aberdeen folk for many centuries, and marked the limit of those Freedom Lands which Robert the Bruce bestowed on the city. To the right of Brimmond Hill lies the valley of the Don and the country road before you will take you down into it by Bucksburn Farm, Bucksburn House and the Mill of Bucksburn, with the Bucks Burn itself rushing by in fleeting cascades through a wooded den. This is B 984, the Howes of Bucksburn road which, has always been a favourite walk with city folk.

Northfield in fact takes its name from having been the most northern of the ancient lands within the city's 'Freedom'. Like others in this category it was feued out and lost, but has returned after many centuries to be once more the inheritance of the Aberdonians.

In a more easterly direction lies Heatheryfold, another city housing scheme which overlooks the valley of the Don and its crowding industrial suburbs. On the way to Heatheryfold one may pass along Berryden Road from Rosemount and through the district of Hilton by Back Hilton Road and Hilton Drive. Here is another area which was once waving cornland. The 198 acres of the Hilton estate were bought by Aberdeen Corporation in 1925 for £22,000 for municipal housing. An earlier purchaser of part of the Hilton farm was the Aberdeen Provincial Committee for the Training of Teachers, who, in 1914, acquired 20 acres. Today on this site stands quite the most valuable property in the whole of Hilton—the £1,000,000 College of Education. Despite all this building Hilton does enjoy an

From the largest woollen
factory in Scotland on the banks
of the Don come the worlds
finest woollen cloths

CROMBIE

The finest overcoating in the world

CROMBIE GRANDHOLM WORKS WOODSIDE ABERDEEN

open-air 'lung' in the area known as Hilton Woods in the Stewart Park on its northern perimeter, around Hilton School and in the still beautiful and spacious College of Education campus.

Leaving Heatheryfold on the left and Hilton on the right, the Ring Road, here called North Anderson Drive, sweeps down to the Don valley and its final junction with Great Northern Road carrying A96, the trunk road to Inverness and the north. Despite its comparatively heavy industrialisation, and an unfortunate degree of pollution, in the river itself, the valley is still beautiful. When three little villages, Tanfield, Cotton and Printfield united to form the quoad sacra parish and burgh of Woodside they took the name of the estate on the Don centred by

SIR JOHN ANDERSON LIBRARY

Woodside House, an old mansion, recently a hotel and now Water Board offices, on the wooded banks of the river. Leaving Great Northern Road on the right, a little beyond the Ring Road junction a road dips down into the valley and crosses the Don here by Persley Bridge, and a pleasant riverside road runs eastward along the Don's left bank through the wooded area called Persley Den to emerge farther downstream at Grandholm Bridge, near Grandholm Works, founded in 1792, and now an important wool and tweed mill.

Although the nominal independence of Woodside, as a burgh in its own right, came to an end in 1891 with its incorporation in the city of Aberdeen, there is probably no district in the town that retains to such a marked degree a sense of its separate identity. Exploring Woodside can be a rewarding experience, full of surprises. On the south bank of the river, for example, is a quaint but picturesque structure with an entrance archway under a battlemented tower, called 'The Barracks'. It was built in 1785 as a hostel for child labour at the Woodside Works, and is now the depot of a sawmill. The building that became the Burgh Hall of Woodside in 1862 was built by subscription as a school in 1837. Another famous local institution is the Sir John Anderson Library, presented to the community by an engineer and inventor who took over the running of the Woolwich Arsenal in the Crimea War.

Woodside is served by the No. 24 bus, which runs in Great Northern Road from the mart centre of Kittybrewster. The name of this industrial suburb is actually derived from Gaelic words which have nothing to do with a lass called Kitty. But William Cadenhead invented a more popular origin when he depicted Kitty Brewster as a kindly brewster-wife:

She sell't a dram — I kent her fine —
Out on the road to Hilton.
Afore the door there stood a sign
Ahint a lairach beltin'.
Her yaird had midden-cocks and game,
And mony a cacklin' rooster,
She was a canty, kindly dame,
They ca'd her Kitty Brewster.

We have now completed our circuit of the outer city. Beyond it lies a countryside full of charm and interest and the utmost variety, and there is a rich local literature on which to draw for further enlightenment on the past, present and future of the region.

The motto of the city is "Bon-Accord" (good fellowship) and its toast is the toast of Bon-Accord:

'Happy to meet, sorry to part, happy to meet again'.

GLOSSARY

ABACUS The top part of the capital of a column, supporting the architrave.

ANTA A square pilaster or column projecting from a quarter to a half from the wall on either side of a door or at the corner of a building.

ARCHITRAVE The lowest section of the entablature, directly above the columns.

ASHLAR Masonry formed with carefully squared stones and with fine joints in regular courses to provide a smooth surface.

BALUSTRADED PARAPET A low wall in the form of a series of balusters (short pillars) supporting a handrail or moulded coping (e.g. as in Union Terrace).

BARONIAL The style of castellated architecture favoured by the old Scots barons in their tower houses—and modern imitations of this (sometimes called neo-baronial) as for example in Balmoral Castle.

BARTIZANS Battlemented turrets on a medieval tower or modern versions of these.

CAPITAL The carved head of a column.

CAPS The uppermost parts of a building or section of a building.

CIBORIUM A stone canopy supported by columns over an altar.

CLASSICAL The art of Greece or Rome or work derived therefrom in style.

CLERESTOREY The uppermost storey of a medieval church lit by a series of large windows and "clear" of the roof of the aisle.

COPED or COPING The coping is the uppermost course of masonry in a wall.

CORBELLING A corbel is a stone bracket projecting from the face of a wall to support a roof truss or beam or it may be a projecting turret.

CORINTHIAN The third and most elaborate order of Greek architecture.

COURSED RUBBLE Rough, undressed stones laid in courses.

CUPOLA A rounded vault or dome forming the roof of a building.

DORIC and DORIAN STYLE The first order of Greek architecture. The columns are sturdy, tapering and fluted, without a base. For G-doric and R-doric see Giant and Rusticated. A Doric colonnade is a series of Doric columns.

EFFLORESCENCE Flowering.

ENTABLATURE The upper part of any classical order. It consists of three horizontal sections, the architrave (lowest), the frieze (middle) and the cornice (above).

FENESTRATION The arrangement of the windows of a building.

FRIEZE See above. A frieze may be enriched with sculpture, hence the famous Elgin Marbles from the Parthenon, the Temple of Athena on the Acropolis at Athens, perhaps the most famous and perfect building in the world. A disc frieze is simply a frieze in which there are sculptured discs.

GARGOYLES Projecting waterspouts, often carved in the form of grotesque heads or winged monsters.

GIANT (or Colossal) columns carried up through two or more storeys—a favourite ploy to show off the massive qualities of granite in Aberdeen.

119

GOTHIC The European architectural style of the middle ages from the twelfth to the sixteenth century. **Perpendicular Gothic**—the third and last style of English Gothic architecture characterised by the extensive use of perpendicular mouldings. **Scoto-Gothic**—the characteristic form of Gothic prevailing in Scotland in the later middle ages.

GOTHIC REVIVAL The vogue or fashion for reviving Gothic styles. In the late eighteenth century they spelt the word with a "K" so such imitation-gothic buildings are usually described as **Gothick** to distinguish them from medieval buildings proper.

GROIN VAULTED Deeply grooved vaults. Groins are the instercises between portions of vaulting.

GROYNES In this case long barriers in the sands intended to trap moving sand and fix it so that it will help to build up the foreshore.

HARLING Roughcast. In Scotland buildings coated in this way are called harled.

IMPALED (heraldic) Two coats of arms juxtaposed on a shield, e.g. husband and wife.

IONIC The second order of Greek architecture; more exotic than Doric, not so elaborate as Corinthian.

ITALIAN ROMANESQUE The Italian variant of the architectural style preceding Gothic and dating mainly from the tenth to the mid-twelfth century.

MOULDINGS Pieces of stone or wood carved to produce an ornamental variety of contour.

PANTILES Roof tiles transversely curved to an ogee shape.

PEND A covered close or vennel (Scottish). A narrow passage usually partly roofed over.

PRE-RAPHAELITE A well known nineteenth century group of English painters who sought to recover the primitive feeling and respect for nature and detail of the Old Masters preceding Raphael.

QUADRANT The frontage of a building forming a quarter circle.

QUOAD SACRA A quoad sacra is a parish for ecclesiastical purposes only as contrasted with a **Quoad Civilia** or civil parish. As the urban population of Aberdeen grew more churches were needed and certain areas inside a civil parish such as St. Nicholas or Oldmachar were allocated to new churches as quoad sacra parishes.

RENAISSANCE Style of architecture developed in the great revival of art and letters at the end of the middle ages. Here it is used to describe the nineteenth century imitations of the Renaissance style in public buildings in Aberdeen.

RENDERED Reproduced or represented by artistic means.

RIBBED VAULTS A rib is the projecting stone or brick arch of the vaulting of a building. Ribbed vaults are vaults with ribs which can be ridge ribs. diagonal ribs, transverse ribs, etc.

ROTUNDA A round building or room, especially one with a dome.

RUSTICATED Masonry treated with roughened stone surfaces to suggest rude strength. Obviously this is particularly suitable to bring out the essential quality of granite, hence the large number of rusticated granite frontages in Aberdeen.

SEGMENTED Built in segments instead of all in one piece, e.g. a segmented arch.

STUCCO A fine hard plaster made by blending gypsum and pulverised marble.

TETRASTYLE A portico with a row of four columns.

TRYPTICH A picture or group of pictures made in three parts, the central part double the size of the two wings.

VENETIANS Windows split into three separate compartments.

VOUSSOIRS Wedge shaped blocks of stone, shaped for constructing an arch.